# Return to You

**STORIES OF REAL-LIFE EXPERIENCES
AND WISDOM THAT WE CAN LEARN,
GROW AND LOVE FROM**

## Julie Anne Hart

First Edition 2023

Published by Forward Thinking Publishing

A catalogue record for this book is available from the British Library.

ISBN: 978-1-7397230-8-8

# Contents

# Introduction

WELCOME TO RETURN TO YOU. This anthology is a collection of stories and wisdom that you will be able to learn, grow and love from.

It is our collective intent that the sharing of our personal life experiences can assist you to identify similarities within your own life experiences, enabling the gift of healing and empowerment to occur. In the giving of our purposeful knowledge, may we evoke within you a knowing that you have the power to discover the potential that is you regardless of the adversity we all at times may face.

Our society is loaded with expectations that can leave us all with many difficult emotions to have to deal with. We often feel alone, as if we are the only person who feels this way. When you can identify with another's experience it has the capacity to create change. It only takes a single moment to become consciously aware. This kind of awakening will ignite your senses to intuitively know that on many levels we are all different and yet the same. We are sold and told a myth of how we should feel or what we should do or achieve. It is our hope that you can strip back these layers of expectations that have governed the dysfunctional thought processes of our families and ancestors.

In the returning to you, there is recovery: recovery from a way that has until now separated you from who you are. May you return to know how to relate more intimately to your five major relationships: to self, to others, to your purpose, to the planet and to the infinite universe from which all is given.

In this book you will read many different life stories entwined with a common thread: our humanness. Even though you may not directly relate to every story, if you give yourself the time to connect to each story there will be something you can gain. Reading this book will have a purpose and hold meaning; it may be that you pass it on to assist someone else who has had similar life experiences.

You will find throughout the following chapters experience and guidance on dealing with health and wellbeing, confidence, empowerment, spirituality, addiction, resilience and birthing your brilliance. Your health and your potential are entwined together in a cause-and-effect relationship. The healthier you are, the more of your potential can be discovered. Resilience is the strengthening of the soul and spirit. Embodying your essence is the knowing of how to use your own energy in a successful way. Lead yourself to know your own antidote within the power of the physical body's own communication system. How you feed, care and nurture yourself can lead to the unlimitedness of a feelgood factor that helps you to maintain health in mind, body and spirit.

Many people feel a sense of disillusion. We are encouraged to crave 'more' of life and yet we already have it. We struggle to find peace or purpose to life and yet it can always be found. Walking a spiritual path is not easy as it often means coming face to face with ourselves. It means taking responsibility for what we experience, as we become conscious of where we are in our lives.

This book is a collective share. You are receiving the truth of our experiences in the hope that it will help you to understand more of the spirit of your humanness. The spirit needs silence to allow yourself quiet time to contemplate. Create a sacred space so you can connect more spiritually. Your environment is an important factor as it holds you in physical comfort and safety so you can begin the journey to more emotional care as you uncover more of what you need to discover.

Nothing is set or given in a way that makes one person have all the answers. We don't. We have our experiences, learning and gifts to offer to you, so we can all learn from each other's experiences. There will be many lightbulb moments of awareness for you to use in a way that creates change for you and for others for your greater good. Peeling away and letting go of what does not serve you to keep doing, thinking and feeling is a reclaiming of your potential.

Living life on purpose is your birth right. You will have to be watertight in your own mind and body as you step into a new paradigm of awareness. The awareness that life is showing you is growth. Your inner awareness has been calling you for quite some time to move beyond your current understanding. As you do this, you naturally take yourself beyond your current circumstances. In essence, you are the one who has put out the signal to the Universe, a spiritual call to say you are ready and willing to learn, love and grow.

Your expansion is what is needed. When you stop looking externally for the results, you seek the spiritual power that is within. In divine timing, the change that you seek will be presented to you. You may be fearful, or you may be holding back, staying in the familiar – but the worn- out ways of thinking will soon no longer fit with the new you. New people, new places, new situations and opportunities will be presented to you as if by magic. Great blessings are always possible. Hold the grace to walk in oneness with faith as life goes through a transformation.

Most of all, we are all here to make a difference. When you connect to the infinite divine power, you are never alone or without anything. Honour your journey and as you do, the doors to new opportunities will open for you. Make your forward movement simple. Just do it. Your inner being knows exactly what the next step is for you upon your sacred path of life.

We cannot tell you what you will gain or what the outcomes will be from reading this book. It is for you to decide; it is in your hands and the hands of divine guidance that has connected you here. So often we are told how information will make a difference; we are told how to change, how to do, how to be. The simple fact of the matter is there is no one outcome or how-to that can guarantee you a formula. Your wellbeing and spiritual journey is unique to you.

When you release the need to control the outcome, you are letting go and letting in the higher guidance of divine love that will guide you to greater growth far beyond your awareness. I believe that the greatest wisdom is within us.

Blessings,

Julie Anne

# The Seeker by Julie Anne Hart

HAVE YOU EVER:

- Explored your beliefs and why you think what you do?
- Learnt to accept what you have been told?
- Felt the loss of yourself saturated in other people's opinions and expectations?

Within the generational dynamics of my family lies the deadly dysfunction of alcoholism. My grandmother left home at 15, fleeing an alcoholic abusive father. It stripped her of everything from self-worth to wealth. My mother inherited the aftermath of alcoholism and so did I. Growing up with co-dependency and control left me unable to make decisions or decide who I was. I met my husband when I was 15; he was 21. Fast forward a decade and at 25 I had married into an abusive alcoholic relationship which I left with a baby, a toddler and a carrier bag containing a few items for my children.

There is a prejudice around women who face homelessness or financial crisis with children. You can be seen as a drain on society for needing help. I became that shame. I battled on, trying to build my empire of education, career, money and opportunities to give myself an identity of achieving. I thought that if I achieved on the outside, I could put right what I thought I had got wrong in my life. I wanted to stop being someone who failed.

Trying to be a so-called successful person kept me in denial of the emotional turmoil inside me. I never addressed the pain until I had a spiritual awakening in the summer of 2000. My life changed in one hour and opened an awareness of a different world. A spirit world. For the past 22 years, I have been on a roller coaster of having to face myself, my feelings, and my experiences so I could begin an infinite journey of change. I believe the route to uncovering the truth is to walk a spiritual path of discovery and recovery.

I have been working through my 'stuff' for over a quarter of a century; it still grips tight on my sense of self. Despite being more aware and conscious within myself, it still takes all my strength to form my own beliefs, free from the regime of dysfunctional family dynamics.

I was told that travel grows the mind, body and spirit, and it wasn't until I had the privilege of travelling into the communities of many indigenous people that the light shone bright for me. I witnessed a different way of living that was natural with a deep connection to the earth. I witnessed a way of leading that was based on the common good for everyone, free from the confinement of the control I had experienced at home, at school and at work. Control of what I should be and how I should do things. Growing up, the emphasis on what I had got wrong was a dominant feature in my life.

Clearing away the misconceptions of what I had learnt is a lifetime of learning to recover. My mind often wonders how I would have been so more in tune with myself had I had the experience of growing up with the nurture to simply be me. To go out in the world and not be judged or deemed a success or a failure. Given a title of average or excellent or not even being anyone at all.

## The Lost Ways

Let us travel back in time, to a time when we lived in a completely different way. When we were not separated from our own spirit and the divine spirit.

I believe there was a time when we knew how to live in harmony with ourselves and others. When we intuitively knew what our purpose was on this planet. A time when we innately held the knowledge of how important it is to protect our planet for those who walk after us. A time when we understood the potential knowledge the earth and the animals graced us with. A time when we knew the sacred connection with the infinite Universe was honoured as a powerful source of unconditional love for human growth and self-discovery. A time when we had not separated from such power, potential and the infinite prosperity of life.

I believe there was such a time, a time when we survived through using more than just our five senses. A time when we had a deep connection to ourselves without labels, stature or cultural and social boxes that create a dysfunction in how we relate to the raw natural uniqueness of our DNA – a DNA that no one else has. This way of feeling, thinking and believing in the self is seldom available to us and segregates us from our very essence, diminishing our power to feel the potential of who we actually are.

In the beginning, was it about survival of the fittest or was it that our ancestors innately and intuitively knew that their very survival was interdependent on taking care of each other? Each individual unique person held skills that enabled the whole community to survive and thrive. A place of mutual regard, where you can just be who you are because that was the perfection of what was needed. When emotions were understood through a deep spiritual and earth-based connection.

A time when those who took a lead role truly understood the needs of the people. When responsibility meant to respond for the good of all and when we held honour and respect for all things. Those times may have gone, or we can question if they ever existed. But what does presently exist is a structure that fails our unique human potential and our ability to live in harmony with the self, with others, with our purpose, with the planet and the infinite beauty of a divine universal power. Spiritually, I feel a shift in consciousness that speaks of being ready to return to a way of being that promotes our uniqueness and beyond.

I invite you to imagine what it would be like if your grandparents had known the persona of your personality before you were born. When you were encouraged to be your individual unique self because that was your purpose for being alive on the planet. A time when you didn't have an expectation to be the same as others, to do the same, hold the same standards and reach the same socially and culturally entrenched dysfunctional goals. Would you not feel a sense of self-worth and self-esteem far beyond our modern ideology?

We become lost in our identity because we have been conditioned to lose our spirit, the pure essence of our personality, to blend in with the masses in a man-made creation of control, limitation and sabotage. Planet Earth has become a place of 'one size fits all' and I must be this way to fit the common trend of thinking. When the very essence of our humanness is to seek the satisfaction of a fulfilled individual spirit, which can only come through our own ability to seek the self. This is not achieved from a stance of ego but from a stance of honouring the freedom to be true to yourself, which releases the ego from the need to place emphasis on the 'I am'.

Imagine the freedom that comes from your ability to own who you are with respect, pride and fulfilment through just being yourself. This level of individualism creates the serenity and security to define your personal definition of yourself. When one's potential is defined only by the seeker, the emotional dis-ease that mainstream society consistently creates can begin to crumble.

Are you ready to have a re-think? If so, it begins with you. Only then can you begin to peel back the layers of what you have lost so you can begin the infinite journey to return to yourself. Return to a way that is natural, powerful and gives you back your potential and life's rich prosperity. It will intimidate those that control, those that place constraints to condition your mind and spirit. You have the ability to seek the true spirit of yourself. The strength to be bold in your expression of truth; to be who you were born to be.

Before you begin to read this next section, I invite you to ensure you have created a space where you can pause and retreat, to simply review your current emotional, mindful, physical and spiritual wellbeing.

Take a few moments. Pause for thought. Take several deep breaths. Clear your mind so you can review some of your life experiences.

I have had to be constantly willing to release myself from those shackles of thought, concept and ideology that prevent me from experiencing more of the pleasure of being alive. I have often found that my misperception is where the pain or problem gains momentum, holding onto the things that bring me down, diminish me and distort my thinking. This way of living holds no value to me anymore and does not serve my highest good. One of the tools I use regularly to clear my mind is meditation and prayer. I ask for spiritual assistance to heal and empower my life and leadership.

I imagine that I am holding a large basket, which represents my misplaced thinking and feelings. I call it my burden basket. I have put so much into my burden basket over the years, the weight of it is heavy. However, I do not surrender it to the Universe or ask for it to be taken from me. I carry the heavy load with me like a life sentence of punishment. Most of what I am holding onto is not mine. I inherited it. I had not realised that I did not need to carry such a heavy load with me all the time. The more I ask for the burden to be released, the more relief I feel. I sit and visualise the basket drifting out to sea and taking away what I no longer need to hang on to.

The baggage we carry often comes into our awareness when we least expect life to show us. Life throws you the experience that gives you the choice to awaken. If we refuse to see the lesson, I believe we then experience it again until we see and feel what needs to change. This is an awakening. Consciousness is a gift. Being consciously aware often leads us on a journey of feeling in a way that raises a whole new way of relating to ourselves. I know I am on a journey when everything is spiritually revealed to me in its own time.

We must be ready to begin such a lifelong journey to clear out the clutter. We must be ready to reclaim our connection to an infinite divine power. A power that you have free access to. A power that heals you and guides you to the right people in the right places. A power that will return you to who you truly are.

It only takes a few moments to enter a sacred space of spiritual connection. When you make this a daily commitment, you are open to infinite possibilities for change. I know in the past I have underestimated such a power, paid no attention to a regular spiritual connection, and yet it is the ultimate assistance that always delivers. Why would I not make such a relationship a priority? My familiar struggle had become my comfort. I knew I was ready to step out of my familiar because familiar behaviours and experiences become uncomfortable and even painful very quickly – as I have experienced many times.

The commencement of a spiritual journey is a quest to seek the spiritual assistance to heal. I've learnt to try and drop any expectations and just allow myself to have the space to make a sacred connection. The exercise below is to help guide you gently to begin making a regular spiritual connection to release what does not serve you and receive the illumination to know more of what does serve you. It only takes a few minutes to do and if you do it daily you will soon begin to grow in self-awareness.

## Exercise One - Release the Burden

Silently affirm the following:

*I gratefully request the presence of the divine power to show me what I need to see and acknowledge. In my advancement, may I know the truth of the burdens I am carrying that no longer serve my highest good.*

Take several deep breaths in and out so you can make mind space for those lightbulb moments of spiritual awareness to enter. Take several deep breaths in and out and relax.

Allow your mind to be free by clearing any thoughts, placing your mind into neutral for a while. Imagine a basket at the side of you.

Bring into your mind, body and spirit the thoughts, feelings, experiences, people, places or situations that really do not serve your highest good. Place them all into your burden basket, hand over your burden basket to the Universe or divine power and ask for the divine assistance to begin to release you from your burdens.

Relax once more. Breathe in, breathe out. Relax.

Stay in your sacred spaced for a moment. When you do this, you have an opportunity to listen to your own wisdom. Messages may begin to emerge through your senses to boost you with even more of your own truth.

Breathe in and breathe out deeply. As you repeatedly work with this exercise, so much more knowledge, understanding and self-discovery can be revealed to you.

You have your own unique power – use it. There is no set way here and no expectation to feel a certain way. Just allow yourself to have the sacred space and, in time, you will receive what is perfect for you to discover.

When you are willing to hand over and try not to control the outcome or seek a solution from your own mind, you are allowing in the power of divine assistance. This exercise has a duality: when you are willing for the old to be released, you are making sacred space for the new to enter.

**Feeling is Healing**

I often find myself in the flow of focusing on the problem or pain but there is no gain in this. Feeling is healing, regardless of what emotion I am experiencing. I firmly believe that feeling is the flow of energy that will in time flow to you many benefits.

I find it interesting how I can become so fixed on the issue, thus losing focus on the gratitude of life in the present moment. Re-focusing has a power with it; it can be invigorating and inspiring, raising your energy to feel different and do things differently.

The exercise below is an enabler, a balancer, that will help you to regain a forward positive focus. A perception of life working out. Reclaiming your focus into what you desire to create will move your point of attraction in a way that can deliver a completely fresh perspective of abundance and beauty. When you take the heat out of the issue and focus away from what you think is a problem, you are accessing your innate inner power. When you take the time to spiritually ask for assistance in alignment with your response to yourself, the magic of the mysterious Universe will manifest to you. It's time to reclaim what is rightfully yours.

The exercise below supports your worth and deservability.

**Exercise 2 - Reclaim the Abundance**

Silently affirm the following:

*I gratefully request the presence of the divine power to show me what I need to see and acknowledge. In my advancement, may I know the truth of what divine destiny has placed in my abundance basket of life that serves my highest good.*

Now repeat the exercise above, this time focusing on thoughts and feelings of the kind of experiences, people and places that serve your highest good. Place them all into an abundance basket. Begin to allow your creativity to unfold through your senses, bringing to you images, pictures, colours, and thought forms. Your sixth sense will work through you in many ways.

Breathe in, breathe out. Relax once more.

## Connection

Creation of anything lies in your ability to connect with yourself, with others, with your purpose, with the planet and an infinite, all loving universal divine power. A SPIRITUAL MAGNIFICENCE of love is available to us all, regardless of what name or label we place upon it. An all-consuming, unconditionally loving power; a POWER so loving, so giving.

In a world of so-called intelligence, connecting to your divine power and an infinite divine power is often viewed as entertainment, woo woo, or, in some main religious bodies, it is even deemed bad or evil. This thinking truly separates us from seeking our all-encompassing creative loving power. It's a place where women in the past have been persecuted for their innate spiritual connection – which is, of course, as natural as our breath. The spirit is our life force energy. When we connect with spirit, we begin to gain knowledge beyond the five senses. When we separate from our spiritual connection, we as human beings often struggle with the encoding of our emotional bodies and minds. Why? Because having a relationship with your inner power is the place where all our answers lie. It's our wisdom.

The power of the cosmos is in you. You can harness your spiritual power through regular connection. It's just a matter of how you use your energy in mind, body and spirit. Take your attention away from your current experiences. Unlimitedness is a consciousness. You will have perceived many factors in life that you may think disadvantaged you or make it hard to succeed in some way. The fact is it is only a state of mind. I am not saying that the journey is an easy one. It's a journey of determination, perseverance and mixed emotions. Adversity can often show us what is needed for us to see. I believe that when we relate regularly with a loving divine energy, it enables the possibility for all that we are to unfold.

We are living in a powerful time. As a channel, I am often told that a divine power is aligning, a heavenly and earthly conspiracy of synchronised divine lessons. A place where we will have to return to a way of being and living that unites us all. We will see a crumbling of class, cast and culture. There will be a rising of potential, a place where many seek, find and receive a newfound wealth. A newfound potential. A newfound purpose. What is profoundly important is how you begin to relate in a different way to yourself.

The past shaped me, and life showed me the lessons. I have the choice to change and transform in the present. Life is the platform from which to learn to grow and have an opportunity to be who we are destined to be. There is no amount of culturalisation or socialisation that can get in the way of destiny. Destiny will be the dominant life force when you are open to the calling to respond to it, bringing forth your experiences that are the gathering of your wisdom. You have all that you need to succeed from the very first moment you took your very first breath.

As I became ready to step out of my familiar conditioning, I had to review the following three areas:

1. Environment
2. Energy
3. Emotions

Take a moment of silence in this space to take several deep breaths in and out. Create a space in your mind and bring to the forefront of your attention the following contributing conditions that may have shaped your concept of yourself:

1. **Your environment**

   The place where you grew up. What were the conditions? What was the culture of your environment and surrounding environs: poverty or prosperity? What kind of environment are you currently experiencing? Is it where you desire to be?

2. **Your energy**

   Were you inspired to be different, or did you conform to your normal? Is your cup half full or half empty? Are you fearful or faith-filled? Do you feel inspired and innovated? Or do you feel stuck in self procrastination?

3. **Your emotions**

   How do you feel about you, your life or your leadership? Do you feel positive and joyful, or do you feel powerless, overwhelmed or underwhelmed? Do you feel your future? Can you envision it?

## Environment

The area I grew up in was a small village that lacked opportunities. My environment lacked the prosperity to provide the growth and development I needed without limitation. The culture stagnated creativity and for me, my environment sadly became debilitating. I knew that where I lived, where I worked, who I lived near, who I socialised with and worked with had to be an inspirational match, a potentiality match. I had to be compatible as much as I could to how I desired to live and lead my life. We do not have to live in the confines or limitations of what we are born into. Driven by the external demands of expectations, we unconsciously learn to give away the power of our own unique choice. Control breaks down the spirit. Control dismantles the spirit of life force.

I am conscious that I need to be more aware of every environment I place myself in, physically, emotionally, mindfully, spiritually and financially. I am on an infinite journey of breaking down the walls of my existence as I have known it on every level. The more I connect in a still silent space to contemplate, the more awareness I uncover about myself. It's not the places you found yourself, it's where you are heading that is important. Your own awareness is the clarity that allows you to focus on where you want to be and the direction you are heading in.

I find that my inner knowing gives me the stability to gather the strength to follow my heart to feel more confident and faith-filled. I can let go to knowing the feeling of what my unseen reality is. As I connect more to my spirit, I can surrender to receive what I am creating in my own physicality.

I invite you to stop for a moment and allow these three facts to flow through your mind, body and spirit.

Fact 1: Only you can limit you.
Fact 2: Your external circumstances do not govern limitations.
Fact 3: You are always connected to an infinite source of wisdom.

Acknowledge how you think and feel about the above. You are your greatest asset. You are the key to lock and unlock doors. You must close a few doors to make space to open new doors. You must be ready, willing and want to take a movement. If you do not, your empowered potential remains nothing but a thought because there is not enough energy generated to form an action.

**Energy**

Energy is a life force, a spark of inspiration, a desire, a passion. It's an inner knowing that ignites the spirit, the source within you to promote you to do something different, to act and to be the driver of your own destiny. Energy is the strength and vitality required for sustained physical or mental activity: activity that gives birth to the new you. To keep our energy vitalised, it's paramount we keep ourselves accountable so we can respond to our own needs with constant awareness. If you can view the spirit within you as a fire, a well of unconditional love, support and warmth that will continuously keep feeding you what you need, then you would want to nurture the fire to keep it ignited. Your belief, trust and faith in yourself will keep the fire well lit. Imagine a place where more life force energy keeps flowing through you. Couple this with increasing amounts of self-care and I have found it cracks the old worn-out ways well and good, to my advantage.

Stress, tension, fear, doubt and anxiety takes energy, depletes the body's system, and produces a lethargic feeling. I often charge up my energy by deciding that I am going to do something and then ensuring I do it. When I make the extra effort to take an action, my life moves on. I have always felt the call to use my energy differently when I am ready for change. Sometimes this is to vision the bigger picture so I can rev up more inspiration to ignite the innovative creativity within me to move towards more of what I truly want to do. My energy functions on a higher level when I am more connected to my soul's purpose. In these moments, there is a feeling of wholeness without the need for evidence. This way of working with my energy graces me with the feeling of fulfilment to take flight into more of the unknown.

My spirit knows. It really is all about reclaiming and redefining my truth.

## Emotion

It's not easy managing our emotions. At times, even associating with how we feel seems too overwhelming, fearful or unbearable. I remember a time when I asked my spirit helpers for guidance as I was so lost in painful feelings. I was quite surprised to have this response given back to me:

> *"If you knew how much growth comes through painful or uncomfortable feelings, you wouldn't be negative about feelings at all. Emotions that are difficult to deal with are more transformative in nature."*

Energy mastery is an emotional mastery too. It's an inner feeling of knowing what is accessible to you in another time space reality. Bringing the intangible future into the power of your now, you are co-creating with an infinite divine power.

For me, it was a confirmation that I might not want to be where I am emotionally, but it is perfect for the progression of my path and destiny. Acceptance empowers inner peace and a vital part of our emotional stability to simply just be and take time to move through an issue without pushing. I think the key is to not stay in an emotional state for too long. I have found I have done this at times because I have been too focused on something that does not serve me. I have not wanted to let go of painful issues. There is a balance in everything we do. Time is a healer.

There is a power in retreating as time assists our discovery of ourselves. Our spirit needs space for expression and communication. If we don't take the time, how can we listen to the power within us speaking? It gets overlooked; it's unheard and unacknowledged. This is a great way to stay the same.

Give yourself time to retreat. The spirit of your humanness requires these following five things:

1. Silence – time out to spiritually connect and envision making the unknown known.
2. Sacred space – clear out your clutter to allow your environment to be peaceful.
3. Stillness – quietness is a quality that creates a connection to listen to your soul.
4. Safety – spiritual self-reassurance guides us on the path of serenity.
5. Serenity – when the above four elements are brought together you are functioning from the power of your spirit, devoid of our mind of myths.

As these five elements of our humanness channelled through me, I knew I had underestimated their significance and how important it is to implement all of them to return to knowing much more about me. How can a divine power infiltrate my inner knowing if I am too busy to connect, listen and communicate with the infinity of divine intelligence?

Magic happens when I take the time to understand what my higher self needs from me. A higher awareness is always delivered to me when I retreat to seek. When you know what your passion is, your spirit will begin to come to life with a new energy and a new drive that will develop a newfound sense of self. You are living life on purpose. When you say "yes" to a life of purpose, life will say "yes" to you. Your purpose is a combination of your potential, your innate gifts, your passion and your life experiences. Are you ready to retreat to seek? The next level of you is always waiting to be discovered.

Create a safe environment. Let your energy be still. Be silent. A place where you can always seek the wisdom to know the action to take. A change in consciousness that directs and creates perfectly for you.

## Exercise 3 - Retreat to Seek the Seeker in the Self

Take several deep breaths in and out. Create a sacred space where you will not be disturbed and allow yourself to feel comfortable and safe. Breathe in care, breathe in comfort. Relax.

Let your breath relax you more. Close your eyes and open your mind to more creative imagery, as you begin to see or sense the next step of your life or leadership coming into your awareness. Make the picture bigger. Expand. Silently ask to be enlightened. Let your senses be your guide. Do not doubt.

Breathe in and breathe out.

Let your intuition guide you into a deep knowing of what the next step is for you and what the divine requested action may be. Increase your self-trust. Stay in retreat if you need to. Here you are not thinking it out, you are receiving divine intervention that works itself out.

You know what you need to do. Do it. Action can be making emotional, spiritual and mindful action, as well as physically doing something. To retreat enables you to take yourself to the next level and as you do, life will present you with another level and another level of you. You are an infinite creator. The more you let your potential out, more of your infinite potential is given.

Sustainable transformation comes through making a commitment to ourselves with the compassion to keep going. I am mindful that my mind is consistently creating. I try to be aware of what I think and feel. We are creators. I try to be determined and have the energy to persist, as I have learnt and experienced that perseverance pays off wildly beyond any dream. The power is in me, and it is in you. I try to truly know it and feel it daily.

Appreciate the abundance of living life in the moment. I have come to learn that fear and worry are limiting energies and emotions. You know some of what your sacred destiny is, so why worry or doubt? A sacred path asks you to see through the eyes of source, a place where everything is always working its way out. To see through the eyes of source is to appreciate the journey of the return to you.

# CHAPTER 2

# The Matrix
# by Julie Anne
# Hart

THE SERENITY OF WHAT WE seek lies in the relationships we weave.

In 2016, I was given a spiritual understanding of how what I perceived and believed created some relationship conflict around me. How I viewed certain people had a cause and effect on what was happening in my relationship experiences. I was experiencing a difficult relationship issue, so much so I really could not cope. I prayed and listened to the whispers of Spirit telling me to rise above the situation to try to see only the spirit of the person and not the behaviour or issues. I was asked to see what was happening from a totally new perspective, a spiritual perspective that meant not only seeing things differently but also understanding there is always a deeper purpose and meaning to what we experience. I was asked to clear my thoughts, criticisms, and judgements about myself and the other person I was having difficulty with.

I was told that, in the energy of perception, all that I assumed, thought and perceived about myself and another is received instantly by the other person in a non-verbal energetic way. The other person can then have an unconscious or conscious reaction to the energy that is being directed to them from me without either of us being aware of it. The body and spirit are fully able to articulate and communicate energetically and will translate this into a physical life experience. Thus, an outcome is formed energetically in physicality of experience. This is the law of cause and effect, and it governs what we experience in every relationship. This is our matrix of creation, the energy field of what we see that surrounds us and goes out into the energy field of those we meet, based on the opinions and thoughts we think.

It is not easy in our humanness to be non-judgemental as our society and education system often lack such a value. Sometimes I struggle to implement the wisdom that is given in a consistent way. I am human and I do have shortcomings, but what is important is having a willingness to stay on a spiritual path. It is about allowing myself to associate with the learnings I am receiving. This is about stepping out of familiar behaviours and thoughts that create the confusion and conflict we often experience. It's about seeing in a way that promotes the best in every experience; not just intellectually thinking we have an understanding but applying it to our lives is the real quest.

To do this takes one hundred percent responsibility and acknowledgement that what we experience in our relationships has a match within our energetic field. When we clear our energy field, we experience change. Everything we see and think and feel comes into being. All our relationships have and are formed upon our own energy, frequency and vibration of perception of thought and form our experience. The quality of all your relations is interlinked and inter-dependent upon you seeing the pure true spirit of yourself and another devoid of contamination of mind. It's a high level of consciousness to achieve, as our humanness can get in the way. I often catch myself thinking the same old criticisms and complaints and then I realise I need to make more of a commitment to clear out the criticisms and dysfunctional thinking. It is a cleanse in mind, body and spirit.

We are all creating, every moment of every day. Our energetic field governs creation. When you begin to feel, see and think differently, your energetic frequency formation transforms itself naturally. We have the power and the potential to achieve an unconditional positive loving cause and effect on everything we touch. We just do not do it. Change comes only through a change within your own matrix of creation and never from looking outside of this creation. One's ability to know one's own matrix is the start and the end of any transformational relationship experience.

To aid your rising into life's synchronicity of destiny, your ability to understand your own matrix of creation is called for in every multidimensional level. On every level, there is a paramount need to see through the eyes of source, to see beyond what you are currently experiencing to a place of divine guidance. To see through the eyes of source is to know that everything is working out for the highest good.

When you see through the eyes of source, which means to have a purer thought form, you are open to receiving more divine power to show you a more loving way. When you see the purity of spirit to self, to others, to purpose, to planet and to the universal divine source, you are connecting more to your own divine power.

I would like to share these wisdom words with you as they have been channelled to me.

## Channelled Guidance

*"That what resonates out from you will resonate back to you. This law is simple and profound. It is simple and seldom reached. For source energy is the purest, the source energy is unconditional love devoid of contamination, devoid of assumption, judgement, criticism and diminished perception. A high spiritual frequency sees only the purity and perfection of spirit. Anything less is to weave a matrix that will not truly grace you with the freedom to love. It may seem an advanced way, but this way is the way of the spirit. This law is simple and seldom reached. This must be acknowledged, and a commitment made to the ability to see beyond any human behaviour or experience."*

To me, it is a lifetime commitment to constantly reflect upon my own responsibility to see with purity of mind and spirit, for in spiritual form there are no imperfections. I must acknowledge that there is always a higher, purer perspective in my human body, mind and spirit with which I can change the way I relate. It's not an easy place to be when my emotions are strong in past anger or resentments. However, whether I like it or not, they are my emotions and not someone else's, regardless of the situation I have experienced.

The more we understand our responsibility for what we put out in the world, the more we can mop up the mess of our mind to create peace, not pain. Our ability to relate to ourselves in an unconditional loving way begins the journey to receive back the kind of relationships we choose to experience. We are all living out a matrix of experiences through our sight that so often governs the senses.

So often, our preconceived energies block our ability to see a different reasoning. To be unconditionally loving is as natural as our breath and yet it has become a high state of spiritual consciousness for human beings. Why? It is because our systems speak a message: society governs whether you are good enough, intellectual enough, rich enough, worthy enough or deserving enough. Trends dictate what we 'should be' and we have learnt to follow and not lead from our own unique God-given spiritual uniqueness.

In essence, we have lost our spiritual connection and commitment to a natural rather than a controlled spirituality.

We are judged, blamed and shamed and so we learn how to continue seeing the same diminished energies in ourselves and others. We have learnt to fear, to resent, to envy, to be jealous, to be competitive, to discriminate... and the list goes no. We see falsely through eyes that do not see any aspect of spiritual truth. We have become the condemner of ourselves and others. We have become the judge of situations and solutions. Our insecurities and addictions separate us from our divine love. When we see beyond the human, the spirit can illuminate the way of truth and create change in unseen ways beyond our current awareness.

Your matrix is a way that you begin to relate to yourself and others, devoid of the ego that formed itself in defence of the way we have been conditioned to live. Personal space is sacred. Who you invite into your sacred space is important. Relationships reflect you and where you are at. When I channelled the matrix, it was only then that I began to consider what kind of relationships I wanted inside my sacred space. How was I relating to myself? How did I want to relate and with whom? I was called to take a good look at myself and what I put out in the world. Was I aligned with my values? So often I looked to others to change without even being aware of the fact that who I relate to is a mirror match to myself. If I didn't want to attract what was in my sacred space, knowing that I needed to look upon myself was at first quite a difficult concept to understand.

When I became more aware of what kind of values, standards and ethos I required from myself, I was more able to relate in a healthier way. It was the start of a transformation to gain the kind of people and experiences that were right for me to have in my life. To attract the right people, I had to begin the infinite journey to align myself with my personality and resonance.

Imagine your matrix is like a spider's web around you, with strands of energy consistently in movement around you and extending out to others. The purer your thoughts, the more powerful your web of creation is in every area of your life.

There are five major relationships:

1.      The relationship to self.
2.      The relationship to others.
3.      The relationship to purpose.
4.      The relationship to the planet.
5.      The relationship to the Divine.

A greater level of peace and potential can be attained when we are in unity with our five major relationships.

Leading our lives with love, compassion and care means clearing out clutter and creating a consciousness that will raise us above the mundane.

Every issue that sparks an emotional reaction is ours to heal; every trigger is a gift to grow. The issue never lies with another; it always lies with us. Relationships, even those we perceive may have harmed us, are a spiritual gift for growth. When we rise above the circumstance, we find a deeper understanding of what is actually happening.

Movement is an integral part of our matrix. We are constantly discovering and uncovering more about ourselves. If you are experiencing confusion or difficulty in your life, it is time for you to make some changes. In the understanding of how you can view your world differently is the beginning of re-weaving your path in alignment with the direction you choose to take.

When you become the conscious creator, you are open to infinite possibilities and opportunities to take a deep level of transformation through your ability to see beyond where you are currently into a whole new horizon. It is typically human to get caught in the polarity of good or bad experiences without realising you have the power to choose to change.

After years of self-help courses and counselling sessions on how to love myself, I know too well that self-love is not a finite thing. I believe there are infinite levels we can go to. Just when I think I am well on my way to a healthier relationship with myself, life pops up another experience for me to look at, to learn more about myself and grow from. There is always another level of realisation that I need to understand about myself, another level of health and wellbeing to discover. Awareness gives me a choice: I can choose to take more appropriate care of myself, or I can choose not to. Maybe at times I am not ready, but the wisdom is always there. It's a journey, for sure. It doesn't have to be doom and gloom. There is a kind of pleasurable relief in uncovering and discovering the unknown about myself.

By making a commitment to this journey, I became more aware of my emotional make-up. The matrix process gives me spiritual and emotional clarity. Once I have clarity, I can better understand my thoughts and actions. The matrix process encourages me to begin to release any conditioned and sometimes controlling thinking. When you enter a meditative state, you are open and receptive to seek the intuitive feeling of you own and another's consciousness. You are in a heart space for new awareness to present itself. Awareness has the capacity to commence healing as well as presenting you with an awakening on what you previously didn't know.

Working with the matrix processes gives you the space and time to begin to uncover the truth that sits at the core of your being. Take a moment to consider how true the following statements are to you.

1. You are taking ownership of your own change and transformation, which comes through a change of perception.

2. You are taking ownership of all your relationships. There is no external projection onto another.

3. You are taking ownership to see the spirit of yourself and others beyond the situation.

4. You are taking ownership of your sacred space; you choose who comes into your sacred space.

5. You are taking the action to achieve a new perspective, which is crucial if you are to change the way you relate.

6. You are taking ownership to commit to continual development that will, in time, deliver a new way of relating.

The matrix is a continual process towards greater self-awareness. Taking yourself through this process regularly is almost like a self-assessment delivered to you by your own spirit. It really is an eye opener. You are moving into a spiritual space, an infinite dimension of awareness. Trying to figure out why certain things happen cannot be truly understood using the logic of your finite mind. Just know that a bigger picture exists and that moving into understanding your matrix of creation makes it possible for you to see beyond your current awareness. Have patience. The spiritual point is to be thankful for all that is occurring now is the grace for your growth.

I invite you to uncover and discover more of how you relate to yourself by doing the following exercises.

## Matrix Exercise 1 - Relationship to Self

1. Gently relax. Imagine you have come face to face with yourself, as if there is another you standing in front of you. What do you see? Is there any judgement criticism?

2. Acknowledge the feelings that arise. Notice any reaction you have as you look at yourself. Now let the self you are looking at, which is your higher self, speak to you about what she or he sees in you. Notice the difference between the two opinions: your opinion and your higher self's opinion. Be prepared to acknowledge this difference and what you may have been creating.

3. The spiritual influence of your higher self will show you the impact of how you have been feeling and thinking and its cause-and-effect consequences.

4.   You already intuitively know what serves your highest good. Make a commitment to honour yourself more.

5.   You will have a change in perception. Be prepared to own the wisdom from your higher self, and, most of all, act upon what you know you have to implement.

When we relate to others, we often blame the other person for having the fault: "If only they would change or be different." It's impossible to change anyone. We can only work on ourselves. When you make a spiritual connection through meditation, you can communicate with another person through your higher self and their higher self. You face the spirit of the other person so you can express in the non-physical realm. The other person can express in non-physicality back to you. Doing this process in a meditative space devoid of anyone else other than the physical presence of yourself is spiritual healing and enlightenment. There is no need for the physical presence of another person. When two souls can communicate non-verbally in an intuitive spiritual non-physical space, manifestation happens.

## Matrix Exercise 2 - Relationship to Others

1.   Make space and time to relax. Imagine you have come face to face with the person you want to relate with.

2.  Acknowledge how you feel about yourself in this relationship. Acknowledge how you feel about the other person in this relationship.

3.  Imagine telling the other person how you feel about yourself in relation to them and how you feel about them. Imagine the other person speaking to you, telling you how they feel and how they feel about themselves. What is being uncovered?

4.  Breathe in and breathe out. Tell the other person you see the purity of spirit in them beyond the situation. Are you willing to clear and purify your thoughts of yourself and the other person? What kind of understanding of the situation is now forming?

5.  Make a conscious decision of what your new perspective is. How do you wish to relate to this person, or do you decide to release and let go of a relationship with love? Make a decision on how you are going to relate to yourself better. Ask yourself, what position does this relationship take within your own sacred space of life and leadership?

The third major relationship is the purpose you have upon the planet. Do we ever stop to feel what we would really love to do, or do we stick with what we think we should do or have to do, feeling that we have no other choice? Our ability to expand possibility is unlimited if we have a greater connection to our source of creation, the spirit within us. Finding the passion to connect to ourselves, igniting the flame of inspiration, can be difficult if the mind clutters the clarity of our consciousness with "I can't because..." We cannot vision or see something bigger, different or new. Our relationship to purpose is a navigation of moving deep into our core emotion to assess whether we are on the right path. A few simple questions in a relaxed mediative state will expose more awareness to you.

Give yourself the time. Time is an enabler for you to discover more of what is held within you. Once this information is airborne, you awaken to the journey; you can begin to process the new information and, in time, sanction the action. The uniqueness of who you are is your birth right. What you achieve with your uniqueness is up to you. You are free to achieve it when you grant yourself the permission to see a higher purpose and thus you begin to weave it into reality to physically receive it.

## Matrix Exercise 3 - Relationship to Purpose

1.  Relax and imagine once again coming face to face with yourself. What do you see in yourself that you have not noticed before?
2.  Acknowledge your talents and skills. What do you have to give to the world that you are not currently giving? How do you feel about your

current work or career? Are you fulfilled, limited, happy or unhappy?

3.  Ask for support from your higher self. Seek through a spiritual request the divine assistance that you need. Know spiritual support is always there for you. When you take the time to connect and ask, you will receive.

4.  Ask your higher self for more information on your next level purpose. Notice what thoughts and feelings flood into your mind, body and spirit.

5.  Are you ready to integrate this guidance into action? Ask for the courage to make the changes so you can be what you are here to be.

The way the matrix was channelled to me gave me an even deeper understanding of the importance of knowing that the first major relationship – our relationship with ourselves – governs all the rest. Our relationship with the planet is interdependent on how we relate to ourselves, to others and to our purpose. When we become healthier in these three areas, we become more sensitive to connecting into the healing and empowering energy of the Earth. By activating our senses, we become more communicative, which increases our capacity to see, feel and sense clearly an ever deeper spiritual awareness.

There is so much magic upon our planet that we seldom see or use. A loss of connection debilitates our ability to activate our innate knowing, which contains the power of our spiritual knowledge. With a growing spirituality, a commitment, and the gift of time, a deep relationship to the earth is an evolver of the soul.

## Matrix Exercise 4 - Relationship to Planet

1.  Each season holds special qualities. A seasonal connection nurtures the activation of the spirit. Do you take the time to attune yourself with the energy of each season? Spring brings new beginnings. Summer is a time to play, laugh and be light of heart. Autumn, a time of harvest, asks us to go within to seek the development of the self, and winter is a time of retreat and hibernation.

2.  We have a powerful connection with the elements. The sun rises in the east and brings warmth, enlightenment, innovation and inspiration. Water brings clarity and purity of mind, body and spirit; it clears the clutter and aids our ability to flow with life. Earth is the healer, empowered giver of life; it's the air, our breath, the unseen spirit that is all around us, encompassing the spirit of eternal life.

3.  Health comes from an earth connection. How much time do you spend in nature? Do you believe the earth is a healer? In nature, you activate and stimulate your senses to give you enlightenment. Earth's energies hold the

power to transform our body's chemistry and emotional make-up. How much time and attention do you give to these factors?

4.  An awakening comes from a spiritual connection. The earth is orbiting in the heavens. The earth is a living spirit that contains knowledge and wisdom. The trees are receptors for the wisdom from the stars, which filters through the branches, into the roots and through your feet to fill your entire body with an innate knowing. This is your deep spiritual connection.

5.  Make a conscious connection. It is far too easy to embody a spiritual connection when all is well, but so often we neglect our commitment in times of need. Commitment is our communication to advance our relationship with the beauty and the bounty the planet provides. The planet is a living purpose. The purpose is to provide you not only with the substance to feed the physical body but also with all the knowledge and wisdom you need to live who you are, unlimited. Why would you not commit to such an amazing relationship?

As we move on to the fifth major relationship, let's take a review on how you relate to an all-encompassing Divine power.

## How do you view spirituality?

Do you view it as intuition? As being kind? As a prayer? Or as defined by the Oxford dictionary:

*"The quality of being concerned with the human spirit or soul as opposed to material or physical things."*

Or do you view it as a shift in priorities that allows us to embrace our spirituality in a more profound way? For it is a knowing that a Divine power is here to support and guide you. To assist your healing journey. To help you lead into a higher conscious way. The making of such a divine relationship builds trust, faith and belief. Without the development of such a loving presence, I believe there is so much loss. Take a moment to honour your own spirit and maybe seek a little truth of how you can relate in a more intimate way with an all-consuming loving power.

For me, spirituality is not a manifestation tool, nor do I name it as my 'superpower'. It is a divine presence that aids and supports my humanity with divine guidance, which leads me to the right places and the right people, to be the best version of a human being I can be. It is sacred, to be honoured and respected.

It's a kind of sacred humanness that is devoid of anyone else or any establishment or body of control. It is culture free, pure, and unconditionally loving. For me, the building of such a relationship is an ever-evolving freedom into awareness and the infinity of spiritual awakenings. A place of continual spiritual growth. Retreat into the exercise below and take a journey to begin to build a deeper divine connection.

## Matrix Exercise 5 - Relationship to the Divine

1.  Create a sacred space by lighting a candle or incense. Take a moment in prayer to ask for guidance and to silently communicate what you feel is important to you.

2.  In a quiet space, take several deep breaths in and out. Feel into your body and ask yourself, "Do I believe in the magnificence of such a divine relationship, or do I doubt that such a loving presence is always working for my good?"

3.  Make a divine request to increase the trust you hold in yourself. In doing so, you move into experiencing more heavenly faith.

4.  Are you ready and willing to freely give your trust and faith to a divine relationship with no agenda other than to build such a loving relationship?

5.  Are you ready to see through the eyes of source, a place of safety and serenity, to know that an unseen divine power is always working in mysterious ways for your good? It may not always be the way you may want it to be or perceive it to be. Are you ready to advance

your spiritual belief to build an ever-evolving divine relationship?

If you answered yes to the above, this is a pure indication of your desire for change. In a world where we have separated from our spiritual connection, we've also decreased our connection with the five senses, and this can block the emotional and mindful flow of wellbeing. Returning to a spiritual way of living is both a commitment and a continuum of consistent development over time. The time and importance you give yourself governs the outcome.

So often, I have kept my spiritual and emotional development only in the fragments of my mind and then let myself forget it. The truth is this is not sufficient to create change within your five major relationships. I must, as we all must, place all of myself into having a greater relationship with a divine power. In doing so, we can begin the journey to ignite our internal flame, the love that is within us, so we can begin to associate with a knowing far beyond the mind.

We are always only ever just starting to break through to feel the deep feelings of a deeper spiritual connection. Even after years of consistent development there is always another level to go to. To feel is the greatest gift; it's the source of knowing the higher intelligence within you.

Channelling the matrix has been an understanding that I too am a creator, a divine creator – but I can only be this if I am willing to move into more purity of body, mind and spirit. After all, this is the essence of creation. Purity of thought is unconditional love and is the basis of source energy. In an earthly dimension, it solidifies as the formation and foundation from which to flourish.

# CHAPTER 3

# Take it to the Edge by Julie Anne Hart

AS A GIVER AND RECOVERING rescuer, so many times in my life I have had difficulty with receiving. Sometimes I have been conscious of doing so and sometimes I have not been awake to my behaviours. One rather dark night when things just felt too hard to continue, too painful to keep holding heavenly faith, too tired to keep increasing my self-trust, when advancing my beliefs felt like nothing was working out for me, I was given some even more direct spiritual guidance.

Beyond your current perception of yourself lies the infinite truth. You are the spirit of infinite potential. You are the spirit of infinite purpose. You are the spirit of infinite power. You are the spirit of infinite prosperity. You are the spirit of infinite unconditional love. The prosperity to feel all that you are and all that is, is the gift of life that lies in your infinite connection to the great mystery, the divine spirit.

When you connect with the power within you, you are the alchemist. It will take a deep commitment with total consistency to follow your own sacred path of destiny, to discover and uncover your truth. It is a lifetime's work, an ever-unfolding evolution.

In this chapter, we will explore spiritual concepts to integrate into your inner knowing to aid, support and promote the return to your own further emergence. Within a societal system that is unfair, unequal, discriminative and dominated by an elite minority that has governed through mainstreams of ideology to control a natural non-attached earth-based spirituality, it is of primary importance that we acknowledge that we all have within us a spirit that cannot be confined or controlled. It is yours to create without restriction of any external system.

Maybe as you read this, you feel a little stuck or stagnant. Do you desire more change in your life, but it isn't happening? The dilemma is we know there is more to our potential and purpose, but we seldom seem to seek it or step out of where we are, physically, emotionally, mindfully, spirituality and financially. If you are feeling a desire to be more of your potential but find yourself asking, "How do I do it?" then life is currently showing you the following:

- You are seeing with a restrictive reality
- You are focused on what you think is missing
- You are resisting the unfamiliar and staying in the familiar

When you begin the journey of stepping out of what you are used to – your past, your upbringing, your concept of who you are, the ideologies you have lived and grown with – magic does begin to happen. But it will take more than magic. It takes you making a discerned decision to place your time and commitment on creating change.

Stepping out of what you once thought, felt and experienced is a stepping up to more of the spirit of truth within you. This means taking yourself to the edge of your own self exploration; the edge of your own reality as you have known it until now. Go to the edge of this reality and seek your bigger vision. Do not stop there. Work with the information that your spirit knows is true and let the transformation come from the depth of your spirit, guided and delivered by a divinity of love, trust and belief. Be faith-filled and watertight to your doubts.

The edge of perception awaits you. Ask yourself what is beyond where you currently are. What do you see, sense and feel? The edge has seven transitions for you to work with:

1. See beyond your current reality.
2. Be what you see.
3. Meditate three times a day.
4. Ease up.
5. Forward focus.
6. Stretch out of your comfort zone.
7. Appreciate both the seen reality and the unseen reality.

Let's explore these concepts deeper.

### 1. See Beyond Your Current Reality

There is a well of potential beyond what you are currently experiencing. There is a spiritual infinity waiting for you to claim. In the spirit of knowing this, you then become a co-creator of your own sacred reality: a reality that is always forming in the unseen active and alive far beyond your current awareness. You must be ready to trust in yourself to hold the faith to know that all will be delivered. Beginning to feel the grand design of your leadership is an expansion of body, mind and spirit.

When you make the present moment powerful by focusing on and feeling into what is in store for you, you are taking yourself to the edge of what is always unfolding. You are not finite; you are infinite in creation. So often we get hooked up in our everyday challenges, and our energy and emotions get coiled up in a self-created collusion of limitation. When you rise above the mundane to see beyond what you are currently seeing, you connect to a stream of possibilities that, in time, has the potent potential to be a reality when you use your own energy more effectively.

A self-fulfilling prophecy is in your hands. The way you use your body, mind and spirit either expands or limits your potential. Put out a spiritual request or prayer and ask that your senses ignite so you may intuitively vision a reality that is a passionate response to living life in alignment with what is important and what you are really here to do. This enables you to get to know your next level self, the expanded self. Begin to acknowledge more of your skills in a more profound way and allow new possibilities of thought to form which, in time, will transpire into physical opportunities.

Be aware not to fall into old patterns of thinking and stay with your expanded self. You will begin to experience lightbulb moments of spiritual awareness as it begins to be impossible to remain the same. New attributes will be revealed to you as your expansion of possibility delivers more enlightenment.

## 2. Be What You See

Be it! Embrace it! Be what you see, the next level you. Meditation advances the connection and the intensity of your inner knowing. Such a knowing will begin the journey of transformation. You will not be able to stay the same. A new persona will begin to form in you. Regular long-term meditation and spiritual development enables you to seek spiritual guidance on what your new personality traits are as you begin to expand your conscious awareness of what needs to change. When this process starts, you will intuitively, innately begin the journey of rising into more potential as well as releasing the old worn-out ways of behaving that no longer serve you. The emotional intensity creates a natural action and an outer manifestation. With a commitment to yourself, you will begin to take a transformation as you will be divinely guided into your own becoming. You do have to be aware that it will be impossible to stay the same. Awareness and the action to carry out what needs to change is the alchemy you gift to yourself. Be accountable and keep yourself in check.

## 3. Meditate Three Times a Day

Meditation is a powerful informer, a relaxer and illuminates much knowledge and wisdom to you. Building a greater relationship with the divine is essential in building a strong relationship with yourself and your inner knowing. Change comes through awareness and awareness is given in meditation.

It's so easy to stay in the same routine. A commitment is needed with the patience to keep connecting to the innate wisdom that is within you in a more consistent way, without any need for results. Looking for results is fear-based thinking. Faith knows – and when you hold faith in a peaceful way, there is no need to seek out the evidence. You know as a matter of faith without evidence what will present to you. Entrepreneurs have this knowing, whether they are spiritual or not. If you follow the 3Cs – commitment, consistency and continuity – success will follow.

Do you believe in the power of prayer? In asking for assistance so much is given; we are never alone and yet seldom do we seek such divine assistance. Advancing your belief is paramount. Weeds grow from doubt and fear takes your freedom. Don't let time get in your way; it's a false premise. You have as much time as you wish to take. Make room for just five minutes in divine connection dawn, noon and dusk. You will begin to feel so much more inspired. Create sacred space, light a candle, clear your mind and be still in silence with yourself. Let the light shine upon you and you will be graced with growth.

### 4. Ease Up

Is the reason we find it so difficult to ease up on life because we try and control outcomes or hold an expectation that is always out of reach? Is life meant to be stressful? Does fear become a factor that can dominate most of our thoughts? Ease up means ease up. Stop worrying. Stop trying to work everything out. Stop thinking, "What if?" Stop. Stop. Stop. Take some time out. It's a red-light warning that we so easily become out of balance with ourselves. In a stressful world, a place where work is a rollercoaster of more pressure, easing up may seem impossible. Faith allows you to come from a place where everything is possible. It's just a switch in consciousness. There are a variety of ways you can let yourself be at ease. It just takes a little self-questioning coupled with giving to yourself what until now you may not have.

Take a few minutes to do a mind, body and spirit alignment.

Know that everything is unfolding in alignment with the divinity of your life. Take peace from this.

Know that the present moment is perfect to present the next level of life's journey.

Know when to rest and ensure you give the time to yourself.

Let go, relax, meditate, play, laugh and work on holding a brighter outlook

The answers are within you. Connect to your heart and let it speak to you of what you can give to yourself that will create more ease and be prepared to simply do it. The phrase "I can't" does not exist only in the fragments of your mind; it simply means you "don't want" to ease up. You can find ease when you look for it. You will also find many more treasures just waiting for you to sanction the action and become at ease with yourself and life, regardless of what is happening around you.

I personally feel that ease also means not getting wrapped up in issues that are not yours or taking on someone else's responsibilities. If you are a fixer or a solver, maybe you are out of alignment with your own boundaries that prevent you from being at ease with yourself. If you are someone like me who struggles with worry and is over concerned about others, pray. There is power in prayer. Communicate and ask for divine assistance to relax, let go and be at ease with life, no matter what.

## 5. Forward Focus

When life becomes too full on, when we become bogged down with stress, overload, burnout, or issues that seem impossible to solve, it is hard to keep focused. But in these times, it's important in your advancement emotionally, mindfully and spirituality that you keep focused beyond what you are currently experiencing. Let go of trying to work things out logically. Handing it over to a divine power means you have the faith to feel into what is in store for you. It is within these realms that you hold the focus on your forward movement to bring the future into the power of the present moment.

You have two points of reality: the earth plane, as you are currently experiencing it, and an unseen reality that is in formation within the hands of a divine power, a universal power, orchestrating opportunities from the intangible to the tangible perfectly for you. You will have to ask yourself a few questions.

- Where do you place your focus?
- Do you get hung up on not wanting to be where you are currently?

When you feel into what is beyond your awareness, when you expand your mind, body and spirit into an unknown knowing, you are forward focusing. You are blending the future into a present moment feeling. Forward focus with faith and you will allow yourself to flow with the synchronicities of the Universe, a place where everything in its own time will present itself to you. Keep faith, keep focus and, most of all, keep the mind clear of doubt as it can distract you and act as a saboteur to your rising potential.

There is nothing more beautiful than to focus knowingly into the possibility of your heart's desire, particularly when you hold a well of love, depth and meaning to the potential within you. It really will deliver the fulfilment of life and leadership.

## 6. Stretch Out of Your Comfort Zone

Let's begin by taking a review of your daily thoughts and actions.

- Do you do the same things daily, weekly, monthly?
- Do you intend to do things you keep putting off and then don't do them?
- Do you stay in your comfort zone and then get fed up that there is limited change?

Let's imagine:

If you were to step out of all that is familiar to you, what would you be doing instead? What is the difference in your lifestyle? What would be your new activities and actions? What would you be experiencing that is new to you? Taking a stretch means facing your fears and doing it anyway. Seek some silence to answer the above questions. Write down several new behaviours and actions that will support you to move into the next level you.

Let's move:

Just thinking it is not enough. A stretch is action based in mind, body and spirit. A stretch is a change in your mindful thinking, your emotional feeling, your spiritual knowing and even your financial consciousness. Nothing is ever finite. You will have to find clarity in your movement and monitor your own progress. It's a journey – but a step at a time leads you to a big leap. The more movement you take, the bigger the stretch is for you. Monitoring your own movement with kindness is key. Drop any judgement or criticism. Let there be self-encouragement without expectation.

Let's just do it:

Move out of your comfort zone. Do something different every day. Be brave and bold. Be prepared to move out of your own way. So often I feel comfortable, but comfort isn't necessarily a stretch. I ask myself if I am prepared to be uncomfortable for a while, whilst I am getting comfortable in the new. It is not always easy. Nerves and anxieties get in my way; I have taken them all with me and found that they do in time begin to dissolve – only to find that I need to take the next stretch into yet again another set of 'let's begin, let's imagine, let's move and let's just do it'.

## 7. Appreciate Both the Seen Reality and the Unseen Reality

Everything is here now. If there is one thing I can share with you from the path to seeking more of my potential, it is that I forgot something. I forgot that, even at the very beginning when it felt like I had so far to go, I never acknowledged I had it all. Not perfect. Not how I wanted things to be, but life was full in a way I never acknowledged, never appreciated. I had a lot to appreciate and be grateful for, but I wasn't, simply because I got hooked up into, "I am not enough," and "Where I am is not enough." If you feel this way, please be careful. The material world can put us in danger if we miss the love and beauty of what we currently have, which is life, learning, growth, love, laughter, pain and pleasure. It's a mixed bag, for sure. The navigation of you and your life is special but sometimes we only see it in hindsight. Hold some foresight and feel with appreciation what is currently here for you. The gifts you were born with and all your experiences have made you into the potential of this present moment.

You have everything you need in every moment. We only think of lack when we think we need something; it is ingrained consumerism. Stop thinking. Stop needing or wanting anything and start seeing what is in your unseen reality. The table is laid for you and will present in ways you cannot currently vision. If you cannot see this, how can you truly feel appreciation? We learn to look at others who have more or less than ourselves and judge ourselves and them. Then the same old feelings come up. Why is it I stress, struggle, or strive? Take these emotions out of your energy system. Clear your head. Love yourself enough to know everything is here now for you in the unseen spirit realms. It really is worth working on.

Love the journey, not the destination. In a fast-track world, everything is instant. We have learnt the dangers of instant gratification, only to find it doesn't satisfy at all. This way of living has made its mark and left its toll. We simply have limited patience and little persistence to keep going. What you learn on your journey is remarkable and it gives you true wisdom for you to share with others. Do not waste where you are. Accept it as a place from which you move on; walk forward and love it all.

Appreciate! Life is too short to not appreciate the moment. When you look through the eyes of source, from the appreciation of your own spirit, you will see what is accessible to you. Keep within the guidelines of your gut intuition and be led by the greatest teacher you can have: yourself.

# CHAPTER 4

# A Spiritual Connection by Sue MacDonald

YOU DON'T KNOW YOU ARE lost until you are found. You don't know you aren't feeling until you start to feel. You don't know what you don't know. And until you are ready to reach out for help, you won't know there is an alternative. **FEAR** ruled my life, but also the acronym means face everything and recover, or fu\*\* everything and run; I chose the latter. Addiction comes in many forms and always impacts everyone around the addicted person This has been my experience of addiction and the rock bottom that forced me into recovery was a painful place to be. I hope you find some identification in my story and can find your own recovery.

## My Story

I didn't know it at the time, but I grew up with two damaged parents who were emotionally unavailable, through no fault of their own. There was no "I love you"; there were no hugs or cuddles. I wasn't allowed to say no, and having feelings was seen as a sign of mental illness or nerves; as my mum would say, "She is suffering from her nerves."

I didn't know then that her father had been committed to an asylum, as they were called then, for a condition that now would probably be known as schizophrenia. He also drank a lot, and she was terrified one of her children may go down the same route.

She had grown up in fear, jumping out of windows to get away from a deranged father, and that fear was picked up by me, not knowing then that I had or why. She had seen her dad threaten her mum with a knife and say he was going to kill her.

I know now but didn't know then that my dad lost his first wife when she had an asthma attack and died whilst on holiday, leaving behind my older brother. My mum has since told me that Dad had said she was never to talk about his ex-wife; it was over, and he had her now. Oh, the secrets that were kept hidden!

I was very lonely as a child, even though I had a younger and older brother. It was like I was unable to connect with anyone or let anyone in. I always felt like an outsider looking in, even in the playground at school and with friends – if you could call them that.

I was a perfectionist, a people pleaser with a fear of authority figures, and a chameleon, being whatever I thought people wanted me to be. I had no sense of self. Looking back, as a teenager I tried to connect through religion a couple of times. I was searching for something, but I didn't know what and I didn't find it there.

I was an intelligent girl and passed my eleven plus, which, in those days, meant you gained a place in a grammar school. No praise; I was a nuisance who now had to be bought an expensive uniform, hockey sticks and tennis racquets, money they could ill afford.

While I was still at school, I met a boy in a phone box. One of my friends knew him but I didn't. He managed to find my number and ring and ask me out on a date. I didn't really want to go but my friend said she would if I didn't. Therefore, there was set in motion a relationship that was going to change my life, eventually for the better, but until then it would take me through some challenging times.

In hindsight, when you look back it was obvious this was going to be a difficult relationship. I had no sense of self, and he had an alcoholic father and a controlling mother who he couldn't wait to get away from. He was unreliable and often didn't turn up for dates; he went out with other people, although he denied it, and was often left at our front door drunk – which didn't go down well with my dad.

However, the scene was set, and he would talk me round and say he loved me and tell me I was wrong about him. The merry go round of denial, and I was already on it.

I did manage to end the relationship at one point and I moved to Nottingham for a while to live with my grandparents while Mum and Dad looked for somewhere to live in Mansfield. I don't know how but he managed to find out where I was. He turned up at the door, again saying how much he loved me, and would I give him another chance?

My mum said, "He must care about you if he has made an effort to find you and come all this way to speak to you." I couldn't say no, I didn't know how – and if he loved me, it would all be all right, wouldn't it? And so began the next saga of my life in a relationship I wasn't sure I wanted to be in at all.

I left school at 16 with two 'O' levels in English and English Literature – because I could do those subjects without trying – and no idea what I was going to do. My mum said I had better get a job or she would get one for me, which really put my back up as I was going to find my own. I asked friends what they were going to do. One said she had applied to the Post Office to be a telephonist so why didn't I? Therefore, I put an application in.

Another was working in the offices at the Hosiery Mills. I applied for a job there too. I ended up working in the factory rather than in an office, much to my shame, until an opening came up with the Post Office.

I had no idea how to self-reflect and look at what was right for me. I just followed what everyone else was doing. I now know these were the feelings of not being good enough, low self-esteem and self-hatred.

This was compounded by my future mother-in-law, who wanted her son to marry an Irish Catholic girl with prospects – and I wasn't any of those. Her disapproval of me was clear to see. As our relationship continued over the next few years, he asked me to marry him and we got engaged. However, the controlling behaviour and jealousy became too much for me and I ended the relationship again.

I was in turmoil. I didn't know what I wanted and couldn't stop crying. I had anxiety in my stomach, which grew over a few days. My mum and dad said I had to pull myself together or I was going to make myself ill; the concern, of course, of having feelings out of control.

I didn't trust myself or my feelings. Why would I? I hadn't been taught how to. Again, there was to be an intervention that would push me back into the relationship. I got a call from his mother, who had never really liked me, saying I had to go down and sort all this out as he couldn't eat or sleep. My mum said, "You don't have to if you don't want to, but you might never meet anybody else." Although now she denies saying this.

The fear and distrust of my own feelings and the people-pleasing kicked in and off I went to see him, not sure if it was what I really wanted. Inevitably, we got back together, and he spent a lot of time at my home with my family. He was pushing to get married now, I think to make sure I didn't get a chance to finish it again, and also to get away from the insanity that was going on in his home as his dad's alcoholism progressed. Although he was seen as the life and soul of the party, his behaviour was getting more and more unpredictable and off the scale and he even turned on his son on occasions, threatening him and intimidating him.

We eventually got married; he was nineteen and I was eighteen. Now I see we were very young to be making such major life decisions, especially as we were two emotionally immature beings with little or no communication skills or emotional intelligence.

After the honeymoon, we moved into our new home, a little terraced house bought from his parents and modernised. I felt very lucky to have such a good start in life and was looking forward to family life and having friends and family around. That dream was soon to be wrecked but little did I know it.

My friend and her boyfriend dropped in one day not long after our honeymoon and I was delighted to see them and show them around my new home. However, my new husband was not so happy, which was evident to me by his behaviour and the look on his face. He wasn't very welcoming and went into the kitchen out of the way.

I was chatting with them in the living room when my husband looked around the door and asked if I would go into the kitchen for a minute as he wanted to talk to me. Unaware of the bomb he was going to drop, I went into the kitchen where he said to me, "Ask them to leave. I don't want them in my home."

I was mortified and confused. I didn't know what to say but I could see he meant it and was not going to come in and see them. That was the start of him deciding who was welcome in our home – and it turned out that none of my friends and family were; only his were welcome.

Again, I didn't understand 'cognitive dissonance', the discomfort I experienced when he had spent most of his time with my family, having meals in our house, watching TV, seeming to enjoy their company – but suddenly everything had changed. He said he didn't like my friends and refused to go out socially with any of them. I tried to talk to him about it, but he refused to discuss it; it wasn't going to happen.

The control was back with a vengeance and anything I did or said that he didn't like was met with silence. He would refuse to talk to me for weeks at a time. Again I was confused. Where was the person who had begged me to marry him, who said he loved me and couldn't cope without me?

One day, I had cooked him a meal and placed it on the table. The table was a drop-leaf, which I had opened and placed the meal on. As he sat down to eat, the drop-leaf collapsed and the meal fell onto his lap and onto the floor.

I thought it was funny and started laughing, as it was so comical to see, but he had other thoughts on what had just happened. "Don't you dare fucking laugh at me!" he exploded. "It's not fucking funny. Clean it up!" And so it began. I shouldn't have accepted being spoken to like that or being treated like that, but I didn't have the skills or wherewithal to cope with it. Stuff like this had never happened in my home when I was growing up, so it was a new experience to me and the fear of saying or doing the wrong thing now became part of my life.

Over the next few years, we had some good times but always tempered with the bad side, where the punishment would come. I was working full time and he was a joiner so, financially, things were good. However, his drinking started to take off and I would come home from work to a party taking place, crates of beer in the house, Irish rebel songs playing very loudly and I would be expected to make sandwiches and feed all these drunken Irish men.

Eventually, when I came home and saw the party was on, I would drive off again as I knew what would happen if I went in and I didn't want to be put in that position anymore. He often went out for, as he said, one drink but then I would not see him for hours. He would return the worse for wear but deny he had had too much to drink.

On holiday once in Ireland where we were staying with his dad and his partner, he and his dad went out drinking and never returned. We had a flight to catch, and I was due back at work on the Monday, so I had to fly home without him.

I was mortified and embarrassed that this could happen to me and told no one what had happened. Only his mother knew, as she had rung and asked to speak to him. He apologised when he returned, days later. Not long after that, his dad went into recovery, joined AA and stopped drinking. However, my husband carried on drinking. The denial and control carried on and it was always my fault that he had had a drink.

Everything changed for me once our first child, Cara was born as I no longer had an escape route, as I had before when I was working. The party would arrive – I never knew when or what time, and as I was mostly at home now I had no escape. I was resentful and angry but couldn't verbalise it and put up with a lot of unacceptable behaviour from his friends.

I had started to try and control him and his drinking, not knowing that it was a waste of time. He still did what he wanted and went where he wanted but I wasn't allowed. I was obsessing all the time, plotting, planning and scheming how I could stop him going out next time. What could I do and what could I say? I was living in my head.

I didn't tell anyone what was really happening and thought nobody knew. If I did mention to anyone what was happening and that I didn't know what to do, I would get one of two responses. One was, "He isn't doing anything wrong. He only likes to go for a drink, my husband does too," so the inference was I was overreacting. The other was, "Why don't you leave him then?" If I could have done that I would have done, but that wasn't what I wanted. I wanted him to stop drinking and be a proper partner and father.

Black was white, white was black as he tied me in knots with his lies until I thought I was losing my mind – which I was. I began to have a feeling he was seeing other people although he denied everything, but in my gut I knew. If I went out and he didn't like it, he would lock me out and not let me back into the house. I would be left knocking on the door asking to be let in, embarrassed again and having to go to my mother-in-law's house to sleep. I would go back the next day, but it was all my fault for going out and he wouldn't speak to me.

One night, he had not returned from work, which wasn't unusual as he would be out drinking. I had put Cara to bed but had a gut feeling that something was not right. My inner knowing was saying he was with someone else. At about 10pm I left Cara in bed and went looking for him. If that is not madness, I don't know what is, leaving a two-year-old home alone. If social services had found out they would have taken her off me, but my obsession had taken over and off I went.

I drove to all the places I thought he might be but could not see his car. I don't know what drove me, but I pulled into a car park in the centre of town and there was his car. He was inside with another woman, and they were kissing. I was devastated. It was someone I knew. They saw me just as I was about to drive off. I went home and chucked all his clothes into black bags and threw them into the garage. When he came home, I told him where his stuff was and to leave; he was not coming in.

I think for me this was the beginning of the end and after this it was downhill all the way. I felt ashamed. I felt like everyone knew except me. I felt like I couldn't lift my head up and look anyone in the eye. I felt like going round to the woman's house and telling her husband what she was doing; however, I didn't do that. Of course, he denied it. He said there was nothing going on: they were only talking in the car and I must have been imagining it. His mum intervened again and said to give him another chance for Cara's sake as there was nothing going on.

I lost my trust in everything, especially in myself. I couldn't eat, I couldn't sleep, and I was totally obsessed all the time about where he was and what was he doing. My head hurt and felt full of wire wool; I lived in my head, playing over and over what had happened and what could happen again. My self-esteem was at an all-time low and I felt worthless, ugly and unlovable. Although my daughter was dressed lovely and looked beautiful, I wasn't emotionally available for her because my mind was always somewhere else. I felt totally crazy most of the time.

If you recognise yourself in any of this there is hope, I promise you, although it is not an easy journey.

## Path to Recovery

My father-in-law had been talking to me about Al-Anon and recovery for years since he had gone into AA and embraced the twelve-step programme. He had stayed sober but banged on and on about it all the time, so I never really listened and didn't think it was appropriate for me. Thank God he could see what was happening to me. He turned up one evening and said he was taking me to an Al-Anon meeting. He didn't give me a choice and I don't think I had any fight left in me at that point, so I went with him, along with my mother-in-law and brother-in-law.

I walked into a room full of people laughing and chatting and wondered how they could be in the same position as me when they all seemed so happy. They seemed confident and outgoing and all I could do was look at the floor. I felt totally worthless. They made us a cup of tea and then the meeting began. Someone started reading an opening statement. Then they read the 12 Steps, and traditions and readings on a topic I can't even remember; most of that went right over my head. I was struggling to see what I was going to get out of this. However, when the meeting opened for sharing, it was a different matter.

These people who I didn't know shared their story with me with complete honesty and openness. They told me what it had been like before they joined the programme, what it had been like when they joined, like I had tonight, and what life was like for them now. As each person shared, the tears started. At last, there were people who had lived through something like me; some were still living with active drinkers, others were not. I couldn't stop crying as the years of pain and self-doubt were mirrored in others' experiences of living with alcoholism.

I had stopped crying a long time ago as I wouldn't give my husband the pleasure of seeing me upset, but now I couldn't stop the tears – and I didn't want to. I felt such relief that I wasn't going mad, but learning that this is what happens to you when you live with an active alcoholic. Your thoughts become distorted by trying to force solutions and you become irritable and unreasonable without knowing it. Everyone was lovely to me and asked me to come back next week, but I was coming back anyway.

My father-in-law gave me a book, a daily reader called One Day at a Time, with readings from Al-Anon members for 365 days of the year. I read it from cover to cover over the next few days, getting such identification from what was being said, such hope and a definite feeling that I was coming home at last. The group had also given me some literature to take away, which again was eye-opening and described some of my experiences exactly: the denial, the lies but also the role we all play – including me – in the family disease of alcoholism, the merry go round of denial. I discovered, at last, I was not alone.

I went back and I kept going back. I knew I had nowhere else to go. I had tried the doctors, saying I was going to leave and not leaving, leaving and then going back when I had said I wouldn't and anything else that I could think of, but nothing had worked. I listened to people's shares every week, getting more and more identification from them but not knowing how to be so honest myself. I was gently encouraged to put the focus on myself – which I found impossible, having spent my whole life focusing on everybody else – and to build a relationship with a higher power; to let go and let God in.

I wish I could say it has been easy, but it certainly hasn't. It has been a painful journey of self-discovery but also a rewarding one. I baulked at a lot of the literature and steps that I read. I didn't think I was powerless and that my life had become unmanageable, although clearly it was. I also didn't think I was insane but doing the same thing over and over again and expecting a different result is the definition of insanity and I definitely did that.

I thought I could read all the literature and work my way through the steps as quickly as possible and then everything would be alright... How wrong I was. I couldn't do this by myself, although I certainly tried, and there was going to be no quick fix, which is what I wanted. It was suggested I get a sponsor, someone I identified with who I could talk to between meetings and help me work the 12 Steps. I should use the phone and talk to people in the fellowship and get to as many meetings as possible. Bum on seat, it was said, head will follow – and that was certainly true.

I did as I was told. I listened, read, worked with a sponsor, and looked at my part in the family disease. I was encouraged to self-reflect, to look at my words and behaviour and to hand my will and my life over to a higher power. There was only one God, and I wasn't it. I was really offended at the honesty coming my way, but eventually I had to admit I did think I was God and could sort everybody out. I wasn't given advice but was encouraged to search for my own answers in that relationship between me and my higher power.

It took time but the honesty I was hearing from members started to unlock parts of me that I had never been in touch with. Everything had been stuffed down as I had been unable to deal with anything that was happening in my life. I started to recognise feelings as others described theirs. I had never known what I was feeling as I hadn't been taught how to do that. I was asked to keep the focus on myself: what I was feeling, what I was thinking, and how I was behaving. It was so hard after focusing on everyone else all my life.

Gradually, I went from being perfect – because it was all the alcoholic's fault and if he stopped what he was doing, everything would be all right – to swinging to the opposite, where all I could see were my faults. I had to come back into the middle and find some balance, something I had never been good at. I had good points too and I was encouraged to look for those and see how my good points had often moved over too far as I struggled to deal with alcoholism.

I came to see that I had taken no responsibility for what happened in my life. I let things happen to me so I could blame everybody else rather than make decisions where the buck would stop with me. I couldn't be honest with myself or anybody else. I was such a people pleaser and would lie my way out of situations rather than be honest and say no. I had been a doormat, letting people walk all over me by not standing up for myself. Therefore, I had to start changing me; not anybody else, but me. I had to admit I was powerless over others' behaviour, but I was not powerless over myself.

Little by little, bit by bit, I started to change my thinking, my behaviour, and the way I treated myself and others. Working the steps showed me how to love myself and treat myself with dignity and respect, trust my higher power and begin to heal my relationships with others. Many meetings – sometimes three a week – listening and sharing with others, phone calls to talk things through with people, reading literature and time spent talking with my sponsor started me on a journey of recovery.

The self-reflection encouraged at the end of every day and when we were wrong, promptly admitting it and making amends, meant I ended every day with a clean slate. Sometimes it might take a few days for me to realise my behaviour or words were not right, but it was like I had someone sitting on my shoulder telling me I needed to look at it. Taking a searching and fearless moral inventory of myself and sharing it with my sponsor also helped. This was terrifying because I thought I would be rejected when she knew who I really was, as no one had ever known the real me – but now someone did and she accepted me unconditionally with love.

Doing this meant I have been able to let go of all the baggage I was carrying. The secrets I had never told anybody, the behaviour I was ashamed of, the lies and also the way I had damaged myself. I was my own worst enemy, beating myself up relentlessly for any little thing and feeling responsible for everything and everyone.

## A Spiritual Connection - Bringing Me Home to Myself

The spiritual aspect of the programme encouraged me to build a relationship with a higher power, to pray and to meditate and to hand my will and my life over every morning and again in the day as many times as I needed. To ask my higher power what his will was for me and to listen to the answers.

Things I had seen as coincidences before I now recognised as this power working in my life and, over many years, I began to trust that I was being looked after. I was now handing over any problems I had instead of trying to force solutions and waiting for an answer or, in some cases, letting go altogether if I realised it wasn't mine to solve anyway.

This relationship has carried me through the years of recovery. Life happens, and we don't always get good things, but the programme and the relationship with my higher power give me the confidence to know I can deal with anything life throws at me. My growing self-esteem gave me the confidence to leave my marriage when I was held by my throat against a wall by my husband, who was jealous of the time I spent on the phone talking to other members and my sponsor. I knew I deserved better and behaviour like that was unacceptable.

Living alone with my two young children, I went back into education, something I had always wanted to do as I knew I had not achieved my potential at school. I sat qualifications, volunteered with Women's Aid and later applied for a job as a youth worker. It was my first step back into the world of work, trying different things as I knew I didn't want to go back into the job I had before I had children. Still recovering, still learning, growing in confidence and able to listen to the guidance from my higher power, which I see as the still voice within me.

I eventually went to university, fulfilling the potential I hadn't at school, and came out with a first and then onto post graduate study. I went into a new career, and I haven't looked back. I decided to use my experience of recovery and self-reflection to help others go through change and stop self-defeating patterns of behaviour. I set up my own company, Introspect and Reflect, to help others on the journey through spiritual connection, change, grief and loss.

## Come Home to Yourself

If you are struggling like I did, try these steps. They worked for me.

Take the time to cultivate that still voice within you. Journey within and make a spiritual connection.

Make time for yourself, pray, meditate in whatever way suits you.

Find yourself, listen to yourself, trust yourself, trust your intuition. You will never look back. The Universe wants the best for you.

## Grief and Loss

Ironically, when we start to feel better, we also get sad because we begin to realise how much we have missed out on, how much certain people failed us, and what the younger version of ourselves actually deserved. The emotion can be described mostly by one word: grief.

Healing involves healthy grieving. There is no way around it, only through it. Thanks to the programme, I realise that grieving is not a sign of frailty; in fact, it's the opposite. Sobbing, wailing, lamenting are all different ways of discharging my pain so I can heal, and they allow me to experience the strength of my aliveness.

You can do it too!

## You Are Worth It

Healing is not a gentle journey. It takes strength and courage because it is not a straight line from pain to joy. It's a cycle and one that must be repeated time and time again in order for us to truly grow. As we shed our skin of the past, we become exposed to the light of the future. We are raw and the fire burns because everything is new. Those parts of ourselves have never been seen by the sun before and now they have, nothing will ever be the same.

And that's beautiful.
And that's terrifying.
And that's healing.
It's worth it.

You are worth it.
You can do it.

Reach out for help if you need to. I'm here for you.

# CHAPTER 5

# The Journey Back to True Health, Wealth and Happiness Begins Here by Lucy Denver

BEFORE WE BEGIN, I INVITE you to close your eyes for a moment and take a deep breath in through your nose and out through your mouth.

*Just breathe.*
*Just relax into yourself.*

Doesn't that feel better already?

We so rarely take a pause anymore, just to stop and consider ourselves, the world around us and the moment we are in right now. We are too busy being hurried along by the demands placed upon us by our work, family, friends, social media, society – and, most of all, by ourselves. We are busy, but not fulfilled. We get used to presenting an image to those around us that doesn't reflect how we feel inside, and we feel cheated for it! We've spent the last decade – or two, or three, or more – following the path that we were told leads to success. We got a degree, a job, a partner, maybe even kids. We bought a house, a fancy car and a fancier watch or handbag. We painted our face every day before leaving the house, kept up with the latest trends, and posed our way through Friday night drinks, uploading carefully curated images to our socials with a clever caption to get the likes. We did all the things we were meant to.

So why do we still feel utterly stressed out, empty and unfulfilled?

It is because this is the polar opposite of what brings you deep, unending joy for life. The polarity of life is important because in it lies the solution.

When you stop to take a breath, how do you really feel? Is there a low-level anxiety that seems to pervade most days? Do you feel that everything is balancing on a knife-edge, and at any moment it could all come crashing down around your ears? Perhaps it is easy to pinpoint the source of the dis-ease: your job, relationship, or an unresolved experience. Or does everything feel so confused inside your head that there are too many thoughts to focus on just one? Does everyone feel like this or is it just me?

Breathe in, breathe out.

I can say this with a high degree of certainty: it is not just you. So many women – and men, and, sadly, children – feel overwhelmed, anxious and disconnected from themselves. Work feels all-consuming, constantly being asked to prove yourself, always a step away from that promotion or pay rise or an extra resource to help you out, but always carrying just a bit too much to seem manageable. You look forward to weekends and holidays far too much – surely every day should be a joy, not just two in every week. Often when you reach them you feel exhausted, burnt out or ill because your body is finally allowed to rest, and your immune system can't keep up. You want happiness, health, time with your family, the career you know you deserve and are capable of. You are capable and deserving of a life without struggle because there is more to life than anxiety, daily overwhelm and burnout.

But where do you begin when it feels so overwhelming and there appears to be not so much as a spare second in your diary?

When you work with your innate Wellbeing Circuit, you tap into your true potential for complete health, leadership and joy. In time, you can harness this potential and newfound ease to eradicate dis-ease in all its forms from your life. It is completely compatible with all of life's cycles and rites of passage, be that work overload, a painful breakup, the journey into parenthood, and even grief. In fact, it enhances your experience of these and helps find beauty in life's more challenging moments.

Your Wellbeing Circuit is lying dormant, waiting to be ignited, and when you work with it, positive change is inevitable.

Breathe in, breathe out.

And so, we begin. Let me take you back to the discovery of the Wellbeing Circuit and show you the potential that can come from being in a place of pain.

When I began stumbling down the long path that led to the Wellbeing Circuit, I had no idea of its power or where it would take me. Being thrown into Post-Traumatic Stress Disorder in 2012 after being assaulted by a male colleague sparked a huge shift in how I dealt with pain and my feminine energy in the masculine world of British Intelligence. I began from a place where my need for control manifested through perfectionism, anorexia, bulimia and self-harm. Not just with blades but with words: self-directed insults and put-downs that reminded me I had no value, this was all my fault, and perhaps feeling this low was just what I deserved. Experiencing a total breakdown of my physical, mental and emotional state led to an understanding that my physical self was not equipped to deal with the emotional and spiritual upheaval I was dealing with. I couldn't see a way through it because most coping mechanisms are subconsciously designed to keep us in a place of familiarity, even when that familiarity is exceptionally painful.

I had experienced difficulties before, but something felt different about this time in my life. I *knew* in my gut, somehow, that I had to break the cycle of dis-ease: with other people, places, situations and, most of all, with myself. I had a feeling that a few months of antidepressants and being signed off from work wasn't going to cut it. I needed to start with my own foundations and rebuild myself stronger, happier, healthier and calmer than ever. I needed to find ways to quiet my stormy mind without numbing myself through alcohol, starvation/bingeing, working too hard and too many hours, or over-exercise (or under-exercise, for that matter). These common coping mechanisms are often accepted and even encouraged in our popular culture. In fact, alcohol is still the only drug where, if you don't take it, people assume you have a problem.

Trauma always offers us a choice between light and dark. It affects not only the physical body; it damages the soul, clouds the mind, and tries to break the spirit. The mainstream way tells us that there is a time limit on suffering and healing, but this only compounds the problem, embedding the traumas in our system and preventing us from moving forward. To truly heal, it is paramount that you learn to show yourself kindness and remove all external expectations of the healing process. This, for me, was the key that made me turn away from my usual coping mechanisms of starving myself, overexercising, an over-reliance on external praise and validation, solutions such as antidepressants, and burying myself in self-loathing. I knew that staying in a place of pain would not help me to heal, and that no matter how much it hurt, I had to do something, everything, differently. It was time to change.

This time around, I opted out of antidepressants (it's important to note that this was a personal decision and not advice – only you and your medical practitioners can decide what is best for you). I wanted to truly feel, even if it hurt more than any pain I had felt until that point. I joined a gym despite concerns I would over-exercise again, and I ate healthily to fuel that training. I sought out a specialist counsellor who dealt with my specific trauma and had a true compassion about her that enabled me to speak my truth and not feel judged, which was something I had been unable to do with anyone else, including myself.

Slowly but steadily, I began to feel pockets of calm and happiness amongst the total upheaval I was experiencing in nearly every area of my life. I learned to have patience with my own pain, knowing that when it no longer served me, I could let it go. I trained as a personal trainer, started writing again, and even modelled for a sportswear brand at London Fashion Week. Before I knew it, I had a whole life that didn't revolve around my trauma. Not only that, I had also learnt to trust myself. It felt like I had been speaking for years but had only just begun to hear my own voice.

I've made this sound easy, but it wasn't. Healing is not a linear process; equally, working with my Wellbeing Circuit was no accident. It happened organically because I finally tuned out the external noise and listened to my internal sat-nav – more commonly known as gut instinct, our intuition. Discovering that I even had a Wellbeing Circuit, that I could hear and feel my intuition, and that living in my truth rather than constantly fighting to achieve someone else's definition of success finally brought my body, mind and spirit into harmony with one another. There is a journey from pain to potential, a way to replace the stress and burnout and imposter syndrome, and every other label and type of diminishment we suffer in the pursuit of what we think will bring us happiness. It is a path that has been lost for generations and it is time for the wisdom and ways to return. Too many of us are enduring and not enjoying life, and do not know where to find the solution. All this time, though, the waymarkers to understanding how you heal, how you manage stress, anxiety, worry, anger, depression, self-loathing... they have been here all along, and you have everything you need to begin. You are the antidote. I am the antidote. We are all the antidote to everything we wish to change, from within to without. It starts here, and it can begin right here, in this moment.

## What is the Wellbeing Circuit (and are you sure I have one)?

The Wellbeing Circuit is your biggest supporter, your greatest ally and your unshakeable friend who never ever lets you down or gives you bad advice. The best thing is that you already have it – it's been there all along, just waiting to be discovered. In this chapter I will introduce you to your very own Wellbeing Circuit, why it makes such a powerful difference, and give you some practical tips on how to begin working with it.

First of all, what is the Wellbeing Circuit?

The Wellbeing Circuit is the internal connection between your physical, mental – or mind full, as I refer to it – and emotional health. These are often treated as separate but in fact, each is crucial to the health of the other elements. Through this circuit runs the energy that fuels each and every one of us and contributes to how we feel day by day, month by month and year by year. If you often find yourself feeling anxious, worried, frustrated, demotivated, depressed, tired, stressed, powerless, angry or simply lost and confused, this is an indication that your inner circuit has become disconnected and is unable to deliver you the energetic signals you need to thrive. This can occur through conscious or unconscious external factors, self-sabotage, or through a sudden shock or trauma that triggers a system shutdown.

A fully functioning and thriving Wellbeing Circuit results from the awareness that you don't have to stay in this state of disconnection with yourself. Through commitment, you can influence and upgrade your physical, mind full, and emotional health.

When your circuit is thriving, the energy that runs through it is completely different. You could think of it as upgrading the entire electrical system in a building: everything looks and feels different. Instead of feeling lethargic, sluggish, apathetic, grouchy or miserable, you feel inspired, creative, innovative and passionate. It feels like a fire has been lit inside you and tasks or decisions that in the past were a chore feel easy and enjoyable. This is the state of being where you don't have to rely on external motivation, praise or input, because you have it all within. This state brings the confidence to trust yourself and your decisions because you are beginning to allow your gut instincts, your internal sat-nav, to communicate with you, and you are giving them the stillness and space to be heard.

## Physical Health and Why It Matters

Our modern lifestyle is not conducive to thriving physical health. Many of us work in a sedentary capacity from a laptop, with our commute consisting of a car ride, train journey, or simply a walk down the stairs. There is also a pervasive notion that physical health is optional, is not connected to our ability to feel at ease with ourselves, and that there is a pill that will cure any ailments we do come across in life. Increasingly so, aesthetics is the standard to which we are all expected to conform, be it body shape, cosmetic trends or perceived lifestyle. Even fitness is viewed through the narrow lens of weight loss or influencer status, with little reward for quietly honouring your body, mind and spirit through movement.

There is so much more to physical health than we understand.

In this lifetime, we are given a physical body to house the essence of who we are. Our senses, character, mindset, all of it is literally wrapped up in our physical being. To thrive on any level, we have no choice but to honour and take care of our physical form. I can honestly say that I have not met a single person whose energy is that of being calm, joyful and serene who does not prioritise their physical health as part of their daily life.

There are three ways to look at physical health: as punishment, for aesthetics, or to support true holistic health. In this introduction to the Wellbeing Circuit, we will begin to unravel the deepest levels of meaning behind our physical health, how it impacts the rest of our circuit, and how we can begin to change our outlook on our bodies and what their role is in our lifetime.

There are three building blocks that create a state of health or dis-ease in our physical bodies: movement, nutrition and water. You can think of these as our primary inputs that determine the energy going into our Wellbeing Circuit: high-quality ingredients (sufficient movement, nutrient-dense food and adequate hydration) equals high-quality energy, and likely high-quality output. On the flip side, low-quality ingredients (a sedentary lifestyle or insufficient movement, nutrient-deficient food and inadequate hydration) equals low-quality energy, and therefore low-quality output. These building blocks impact not just how we feel physically, but how we respond mentally and emotionally, too – *because our level of physical health determines our chemical and hormonal balance, which controls our ability to process thoughts and emotions*. Simply put, not only do we need our physical health to deal with stressful situations, anxiety, and more complex emotions, these are all less likely to occur at all if we have resilient physical health.

When we choose to see physical health as an essential ingredient for a stress-free life, it can feel daunting. Do I have to join a gym? Can I ever eat cake again? What if I really like wine and think water is boring to drink? These questions stem from a place of fear and when we recognise this, we can accept that they won't help us get to where we want to be. The body knows what it needs to be in a state of health, and it is often a simple need such as water, vitamins and minerals which are essential to our cellular makeup. It is the mind that leads us astray and complicates matters with its ego-based energy.

When we realise that our physical health is a necessity, we can see it from the perspective of: "What will make me feel better in this moment and future moments?" Although the mind may crave a quick fix (a glass of wine, a visit to see an ex, or a third helping of doughnuts), when you listen to it, your body will be asking for what it needs to quiet the mind and dissolve your stressors. This may be a gentle walk or an intense HIIT session. Every person and every situation are different. The secret is to listen to your body and not to your mind, so you can feel more connected to yourself again.

## Mind Health - From Mind Full to an Ocean of Calm
*From Scarcity to Abundance*

Mental health has become a mainstream topic over the last decade, and rightly so. Gone are the days of it being treated as second fiddle to your physical health, and there are now many dedicated services offering guidance and support if you are struggling.

Having said that, our mental health is rarely discussed in the context of our physical or holistic health. We have already learned that we can alter the chemical and hormonal balance in our bodies through positive movement, nutrition and water intake, and so too do these shift the electromagnetic frequencies that makes up our brainwaves. That change has a huge impact on our ability to process and manage stress. If you liken your state of mind to waves on an open sea, then a mind filled with stress, anxious thoughts, worry, frustration, anger, or a feeling of lack would resemble a stormy sea with tall, fast-moving and closely-packed waves. The polar opposite of this is a calm, peaceful mind with space for clarity of thought, joy and a feeling of contentment, or an ocean of calm. So, how do we achieve this?

The first step begins with focusing on our physical health. Why? Moving our bodies in whatever way feels good – be it dancing, running, weightlifting or walking – allows our minds a chance to empty out any negativity that may have built up during the day or week. Fuelling our body lessens the overall stress on our circuit, giving it the best possible chance to work optimally. You know you wouldn't perform at your best in an exam/race/big presentation if you'd been on a weekend bender the night before. The same principle applies here.

Sometimes, the stress levels are too high to clear through simple movement alone. There are too many techniques and too much wisdom to go into detail here, but one key technique central to a healthy circuit is how we breathe.

Breathing is our first and most basic human need, but how often do we stop and pay it any attention? We notice it only when we don't have enough: when the air is thin at high altitudes; during a tough workout or run; when we're learning to swim underwater. The rest of the time, we tend to forget about it, but it is the most essential part of what makes us living, breathing humans.

Have you ever stopped to wonder what would happen if we paused every now and then to honour the breath in and out of our bodies? This is one of the quickest and simplest ways to bring about that ocean of calm to a stressed-out mind. Why is this not something we all do, every day? I'm inclined to think it's because of its simplicity and accessibility that we overlook its power. In our culture, we expect to pay handsomely for solutions to stress, health and wellbeing, but our breath is something we can tap into for free. In the Practical Tips section below, you can download the Retreat Breathing Method: the foundation breathwork that you can access anytime, anywhere, whoever you are.

## Emotional Health - the Forgotten Art of the Senses

In Western culture, emotions are something over which we have no control; they flux as they please and are unconnected to the macro state of our overall wellbeing. We might feel happiness, sadness, excitement or frustration driven by the events of the day, but how much do we understand about exactly what creates an emotion, and how we can spend more time towards the happier, calmer end of the emotional scale?

Let's begin with how we perceive emotions. How do we experience the world around us? Through our senses: touch, taste, smell, sight and sound. When we think about the things that make us feel happy, sad, excited, frustrated (or any other emotion), they are all things that we *have to* experience through one or more of our senses. It's also possible for two people to experience the same event and respond in completely different ways. We all know that person who has a negative comment about *everything*. By understanding and working with your circuit, you will increase your chances of seeing the good, staying calm even in usually stressful situations, and, with some practice, not letting other people's negativity affect your mood!

Now we can see that our perceptions are not fixed by external events but determined by our reaction to them: the word 'emotion' is the giveaway: *e-motion* or, in fact, *energy in motion*. Our senses and, therefore, our emotions are designed to flow like water, and all the techniques we have already covered – movement, good nutrition and water intake, and breathwork – contribute to the likelihood that we will perceive the world in a positive, calm way.

## Energetic Health - Trusting Your Instincts

When you apply this wisdom and understanding of how your circuit functions, it gives you complete freedom to manage stress, anxiety, worry, self-doubt or any negative thoughts or feelings you might have. The results are astonishing: like a bulb suddenly lighting up because the circuit board has been wired correctly, or a clear road on a long journey. When your Wellness Circuit is functioning optimally, everything seems easier and less cluttered with unwanted drama or stress. Life with a thriving Wellbeing Circuit is like suddenly having access to a sat-nav that will always guide you to the best destination for you at any time, anywhere and in any situation. The sat-nav in this instance is your gut instinct. Instincts not only kick in when you need to go into fight, flight or freeze mode but they are there all the time, waiting for you to hear them. By clearing the clutter from your Wellness Circuit, you allow the signal through loud and clear! What better way to live, love and work than never needing to question your decisions, and feeling joyful and stress-free no matter what life throws at you. With The Wellbeing Circuit method, it's easier and closer than you think.

## Practical Tips

When you work with me, you will be guided through the processes and tailored techniques to connect your Wellbeing Circuit. To get you started, what tips can you begin integrating straight away to improve your state of physical, mental and emotional health and move you closer to that ocean of calm?

1. ***Improve your physical health***
   - Include a form of movement in your day. Before you begin, take a pause and breathe into your body: how does it want to move? Take your ego out of the equation and do what feels right. This could be dancing, walking, running, cycling, HIIT, weight training, yoga, boxing, swimming, tennis or team sports such as netball or football. Anything you enjoy that increases your heart rate and makes you breathe more heavily is giving your Wellness Circuit a real boost.

   - Keep a bottle or glass of water nearby and stay hydrated. A simple way to work out the minimum you need per day is: your bodyweight in kg x 0.033. If you exercise, drink caffeine or alcohol, or are unwell, you will need to increase this amount. If you feel dehydrated, try adding an electrolyte tablet to your water, as ensuring your electrolytes are balanced is essential to feeling well. Water is simple but a hugely underestimated healer and contributor to our cellular health.

**2. *Improve your mental health***

- Practice kindness through your breath. Many people are great at helping others but not so good at taking care of themselves, and this is an important component of your Wellbeing Circuit. Your mind activates what is already in it, so the more positive inputs it receives, the less negativity and stress have a chance to fill it up. The breath is your pathway to a clear mind and access to your internal sat-nav. Try to make time for eight minutes of breathwork each day. You can download the beginner's breathwork, Retreat Breathing Method, link in my About Author section at the back of this book.

- As with anything, commitment is key. Use the Retreat Breathing Method every day for the next 30 days and see how much more connected you feel!

**3. *Improve your emotional health***

- Your emotions are directly linked to your senses. Develop self-awareness around your sight, smell, sound, touch and taste and aim to experience as much positivity through your senses as you can.

- Notice when you feel you might be taking on other people's emotions (negative or positive). Even taking two to three deep breaths can be enough to break the pattern and stop their stressful energy from entering your Wellness Circuit.

## What next?

The feeling of being in complete alignment with your inner self is unmistakable. It may take some time to achieve, depending on how deep the dis-ease runs, and how often you are being asked to live in misalignment (for example, a job you strongly dislike or find very stressful, or being around negative personalities on a regular basis). Over time, you will come to hear when your body and your gut are speaking to you and how to listen to what they need to thrive.

This can often cause great shifts in priorities, from feeling that keeping up with societal expectations, fashion and popular culture are the most important things in the world, to feeling that you will no longer compromise your health for the sake of a few popularity points. You do not need to fear this change. When we remember that the mind activates what is already in it, the more we emit the higher frequencies that occur naturally when we are in alignment with our true selves, the more we will attract to us what we need to remain in alignment.

The body, the emotions, the gut all want to be in calm and in balance. This dis-ease only results when we go against our instincts and instead listen to the myths of the mind.

It can be a fearful prospect, tuning out the noise around us and daring to go against the mainstream. We are so used to being expected to put up with overwork, overwhelm, anxiety, stress and burnout that the thought of turning our backs because we have found a new path of ease can feel almost wrong. Aren't we told that everything worth having is hard to achieve? Aren't we shown that we need to be first in the office and last home, the one who shouts the loudest, the one who can guarantee the outcome, the best salesperson, in order to be successful? Igniting your Wellbeing Circuit is just the start of turning your pain into potential and becoming abundant in every area of your life. Disconnecting from the expectations and perceptions of others may be hard because we are so conditioned to believe they are important.

Once you have learned to tune into the intelligence that lies within your body, your journey away from stress and towards true health, wealth and happiness is only just beginning.

# CHAPTER 6

# Now I Know the 'Self' by Buckso Dhillon-Woolley

AS A MIDDLE CHILD OF six children born to first generation Indian parents here in the UK, I guess I was predestined to have a need to be seen and heard. Even though, being female in this culture, the very idea of that was not likely to be met with any support!

I realise only now, after losing my father in January 2020, exactly who I am, hence the reason this chapter is titled as it is. I also realise there are lots of women, hurtling towards 50, who DON'T know who they are, and maybe haven't even started to scratch the surface to find out. I thought it would come from expeditions to far flung countries, or having lots of different experiences, wild nights out. But I find only now, once I truly went to the 'Mariana Trench' of my soul, do I know what it is to know thyself. This is the hope I have for you reading this, that you too will be inspired to want to know the truth of who you are and to know yourself.

Irrespective of the fact that I was born into a first-generation Indian immigrant family, I feel there is a common denominator that all we women will have felt which is not necessarily decided just by culture. I think it's safe to say that a lot of us out there have this feeling within us of being unfulfilled. You may be feeling this right now.

We have this feeling of needing to know more. We have this belief that we are constantly being judged and 'decided for', irrespective, like I say, of which culture we are in.

You may be reading this right now feeling that you never wanted to settle for mediocrity, never wanted to settle for anything LESS than, but were somehow herded into that corner of life. When did it happen?

Which moment in life, or sliding doors moment in life, created that possibility for you? In fact, let's take it one step further. How many decisions that we made in life were actually as a direct result of us doing what we wanted to do, knowing the truth of who we were? When did we just 'go with the flow' because we wanted an easy life and didn't think there was another option for us? I can remember from a young age always asking "Why?" when something was presented to me that I was told I couldn't do. The answer would always come back as "Because Indian girls don't do that."

However, I still wanted to know why because that wasn't enough of an answer for me. It didn't satisfy me. I was always left feeling unfulfilled. I was doing this before I had any knowledge of what it was to speak your truth. I just had this inherent feeling, a need to know the truth, that things had to be right.

If they didn't sound right to me, I would have to challenge them. Maybe I should have been a lawyer; maybe I was a person for liberty in one of my past lives! In fact, I do actually have a huge passion for justice. Whenever I am out and about, socially, and somebody is being mistreated or something isn't right in the way balance needs to be restored, I automatically feel I need to restore the balance. If you imagine going through life like that, you eventually give all your power away because you're always looking externally to make things right. Constantly looking outward to what it is that needs to be fixed in order to make you feel better.

Now, a part of this process has become apparent to me that, when one really gets to know the Self, that is when everything makes sense. But is there a right time in life when one discovers oneself, or does it happen exactly when it's meant to?

The 28th January 2020 is a date that's forever etched in my mind, a date that my life took a turn for.... the *best*. My father, the man I had based all my life decisions on (I now realise), made his transition from this earthly plane after his health started to decline three months prior. "As long as I get to 75, I'll be happy," he said, after his 70th birthday. Six months before he turned 75, he passed. Not bad. I think I will be incredibly happy if I should manage to miss my desired expiration date by only six months. This event was the start of what I can only describe as a life changing moment as, unbeknownst to me, it was to be the start of *my* end. The end of *me* as I knew it.

My relationship with Dad was not what you would call healthy. As the middle child of six, growing up Dad constantly lamented that, "If only you had been a boy" life would have been so much easier for them/us all. It was always said with affection or with pride, as he boasted about my unbelievable strength (for a girl) as I would haul a 55kg sack of 'taters' over my shoulder and into the shop.

Most of my early life from the age of 9 and 10 had me playing some part in whatever business he was running at the time, always hating it despite it probably being the most important lessons in discipline I would ever have. I had always been the 'rogue' of the litter, never conforming, always off on my own trail, which never really changed the older I got. I would always have to question *everything* that was presented to me, querying the do's and don'ts of what a Punjabi girl did or didn't do. Despite leaving school with no qualifications, I wanted answers to why I couldn't go to college, and why should I end up with a thick, Danny Devito lookalike as a husband just 'cos I was slightly chubby and short with no qualifications?!

I don't think that's unreasonable to want to ask, is it? Joking aside, it really was a thorn in my side as I grew up and I became determined to live life MY way and not the way of a culture passed on through generations and never questioned. Don't get me wrong now, I had the utmost respect for those who were happy in their space and I never disrespected my parents around their beliefs and desires, but the minute I had the opportunity to forge my own path, I jumped on it! You could say I kind of knew myself already at that age.

I realise now that my pops had a lot of expectations that he put on me – on all of us, in fact. As with any situation in which we do this thing where we put an expectation or attachment onto a desired outcome, we WILL most definitely be met with

failure as we are wanting people, places and things to
be different to what they are.

I was never going to meet my father's
expectations, which kind of saddens me now to think
about, because I realise I was trying to take on their
hardship and *fix it*. But now I know how detrimental
to our mental health that can be, even in all its
innocence, because we then start a process in life of
wanting to control the destiny of others under the
guise of 'betterment'. Instead, all we are doing is
trying to create an environment that makes us feel
better which, in turn, seeps into our adult life.

When Dad died, I never in a million years thought
it would result in what I now know to be my spiritual
awakening and 'ego death'. This is why I referred, at
the start, to his passing also being the death of me, the
ego part of me that was still lingering. As far as I was
concerned, I was a spiritual being, already 'awake' and
tuned into what the afterlife meant for us and where
we were headed etc. I thought I was pretty locked
down on all of that – but NO! Boy, did I get that
wrong! As the months passed, I realised I had this
nagging questioning in the back of my mind (you
know, that part of me that I thought only showed up
during my rebellious teen years – well, it came back
and I wonder now if that was actually my Higher Self,
even then, communicating avec moi), wanting
answers again to this one, burning question.

### What the hell am I doing here and who the F*CK am I?

When we die, a fair few of us choose cremation as a means to complete the circle of life and within the Sikh culture it's no different. It's the thing to do, after transitioning. As I saw my dad's coffin go into the incinerator (my first one ever at 48, never having lost anyone close to me), a thought came into my head; or was it a thought? We could do that 'thing' where folks create a diamond out of their loved one's ashes by growing it in a lab for 10 months or so and making a necklace or ring out of it, as a keepsake. Hmmm, that would be nice, wouldn't it? But then it got me wondering. How was that scientifically possible? Which led me to research a few bits. I learned that when we die, our bones hold around 1-3 grams of carbon, which is the main constituent of a diamond forming, and that meant only one thing to me, in that moment of realisation.

### Why do we have to die in order to reveal the diamond within?

I mean, come on! Metaphorically speaking, we have the ingredients of a bloody diamond in us! Why aren't we shining bright in our god given TRUE brilliance??! Why aren't we showing *all* our many facets that make us unique in our brilliance, just like a priceless gemstone would? This was just such a WOAH!! moment for me because I recognised there and then the pure wisdom and knowing in that 'message' I had received from source/higher self, whatever you like to call it (maybe Dad!) that it had to have some meaning to it. Maybe this was the way we got to 'know the self'?

Therefore, 2020 became very much a journey of self-discovery, a DEEP need to KNOW the self and find out really just what it is and what I was meant to be doing here, in this lifetime.

The way I saw it, looking at my Dad's timeline:
1) 1962, hits the shores of England aged 17, has a year here, hates it and goes back to India.
2) Returns a year later after marrying my mother. Six kids come along between the years 1967-1977.
3) Works in varying roles, mostly self-employed, never making much money (I don't think!).
4) Retires from the workplace he first worked in as a youth (talk about full circle).
5) Passes away nine years later.

Now, when I looked at his timeline like that, the basic rawness of it, I recognised that that just *wasn't* good enough. What was that all about, man? I needed more answers. I wanted to know REALLY what I HAD to do while I was here because in 21 years I was going to be eligible for state pension and then and then... time wouldn't be on my side! I would never get to do what I am supposed to do or meant to do.

Joking apart, this is how 2020 got me. Pain raged through my body as I regenerated from the years of trauma, self-sabotage, negative self-talk, et al that I had subjected it to. Most days I was unable to walk properly and dress myself, therefore I lived in my housecoat-cum-dressing gown and as for seeing the sun and getting my vitamin D fix – well, I would spend sunny days lying on the lawn with a blanket over me like some octogenarian, with my healing music next to me playing out of my phone. That was the best I could muster, although, you know, the one good thing to have come out of that little exercise was LOVE! You see, having lived in our house for nearly 22 years I had always hated our garden but, I tell you what, after the lockdown summer we had, I'm now pleased to say I've a newfound love for it and a deep appreciation of the beauty and solace it served me during such a difficult yet rejuvenating time in my life. This seemed to be the theme though. The sheer depth of everything I was experiencing was taking me further into myself and the more I surrendered, the more I connected deeper unto the part of me that was in a space and place of pure consciousness without fear, scarcity, lack or judgement. Maybe it was the Higher Self?

As I look back, I know I am still going through this deepening process and I've since felt compelled to help others through their own awakenings. I have created a spiritual development programme currently called 'Discover Your Diamond Blueprint'. I say currently because I seem to be changing in my outlook from week to week! I change my social media bios, like, every week! But you know what? It's okay. It's all good because all you need to do is get started. Relinquish all control and the need to know what's coming next.

What I know for sure is that we DO have a *thing* that happens to us when grief appears. A switch that *flicks*. This is something that can come from a myriad of things that expire or end abruptly. Aside from the understandable passing of loved ones that we grieve for, we grieve when we aren't required so much by the kids, as they move on to uni etc. I mean that in the basic sense of what being mummy was all about with them as babies and growing up. We also have to deal with the end of that amazing job we loved and now have to leave because it's time to retire, even though you still feel like you could stay another 10 years. However, you don't – because society dictates that NO, it's time to go now; go and enjoy retirement, you silly bugger! As if that's really what we should be aspiring to do.

No one tells you at 20 that when you hit 40/50 years old you're still gonna have the thoughts and feelings of your 30-year-old self.

What about the grief one feels at the death of their old self? Or ego? Yep, it's actually a thing. This is exactly what I went through in 2020 when I realised my identity was shifting. I was shedding my ego self – that part of me that had, thankfully, been keeping me functioning through my turbulent life and had given me the survival mode I so needed in order to go forward. Therefore, when it came to letting go of it, it was a sad moment, a time for me to grieve because this had been an integral part of who I was and had been for the best part of 30 years. It was like an old, trusted friend that I was parting company with. There's a time for mourning in that too. The ending of anything brings about an opportunity for us to recalibrate our inner sat-nav, in my opinion. It's a great time for us to really listen to our body and see just what it is that the very essence of us, our soul, truly wants us to do in order that we may live our lives on purpose, doing just what it is that we are meant to be doing. This is where getting to know thyself really comes into play.

No one tells us that if we do our inner work and go forward in life thinking good thoughts, doing good things, being around good people, we'll THRIVE! Yes, we learn this stuff as we get older – but imagine if it was taught to us as kids? Imagine if our parents had taught us real wisdom instead of just things they'd been told or had experienced. Once we know this, it becomes our duty to educate ourselves around it; as I once read somewhere, in this day and age there is no excuse for us to be ignorant. We have so much info at our fingertips and it's our duty to find out our truth.

### *Grief is a golden opportunity to recalibrate our inner sat-nav.*

Yeah, you read that right. Again, this is my opinion and experience from getting to know MY self. I'm sharing this here with you in the hope that someone somewhere will be inspired to take action and start their process of self-discovery, just like I did.

Speaking *your* truth really comes to pass once you heal all (or as much as you can) of your past emotional traumas. This was something I did over six months from 20 October to 21 March, and I continue to chip away at the bits that rise up from the very deep places, as and when they choose to appear. I never once played victim or was surprised by anything and you know, that is SO liberating; I can't begin to tell you how it feels! Try it for yourself!

The pure potential of my future is stretching out before me and it's this that I wish for everyone to see, feel and have for themselves so they too can live their life of fulfilment knowing the truth of who they are.

You never need to make another person wrong or hand over power to an outside source or rely on external factors to heal you because, once you get to know yourself, these things just melt away into the ether. These things stop having a hold on you. These things we came to rely upon so much no longer have the same attractive lustre that once held us captivated. Wow! Empowerment, right there.

It could be your step in the right direction.

Always in Truth and Light.

# CHAPTER 7

# Embody Your Essence by Katy Henry

IN A WORLD FULL OF social media, promises of the next 6-7 figure launch, shoulds, if onlys, flashy shiny objects, fear of missing out and comparisonitis, there is huge pressure on us as members of the human race to do more and be more. I am Katy Henry, a five-element acupuncture practitioner, intuitive mentor and business owner. Whilst the temptation to go in search of the next course, coach, 'fix me' solution is real, I am here to invite you to stop for a moment, take a breath and connect deep into your soul, for everything you could possibly want or need is within you.

It's time to start trusting your body again and listening to the whispers of your soul.

Not so long ago, whilst I was busy living my best life, loving my work as a fertility acupuncturist, helping people create their dream families, building my natural healthcare business, supporting complementary health practitioners build their dream practice and helping countless people out of pain and into better health, there was a time when things shifted within me. I couldn't really tell you the moment it started, but the joy, the purpose, the passion was slowly starting to slip away. I wasn't too sure where the magic had gone, but I held on for far too long, too unsure of what might happen if I let go, even just a little bit, and trusted my inner knowing. What had changed was that whilst I knew the joy my patients were experiencing as their much longed-for babies were born, I had a little emptiness inside as it no longer brought me the same level of joy or satisfaction. The unthinkable had happened (or so I thought at that time): my 'purpose' in life had disappeared, the very thing that had given me such a shift and change in life to help me move through years of depression and suicidal thoughts. A vocation I was proud of, that created the most positive impact in people's lives that I could think of, no longer filled my heart with joy. It no longer felt like my 'path'...

Therefore, I began to search for the illusive feeling of fulfilment in doing more, striving for more and 'being more' – all my efforts and investments of time and energy in coaches and courses leaving me more exhausted and frustrated than before. Until one day I stopped, as my body and mind craved rest. My spirit craved adventure, so I bought a motorhome, a beautiful puppy and took off on a road trip that I named 'No Plans or Expectations' – beyond knowing I was heading to the south of Portugal and Spain. I went with an open heart and a curiosity to feel what it was like to live more in the moment. As I unwound from the years of living in 45-minute appointments, I found the beauty of spaciousness and I started to hear the whispers of my soul.

Working with my inner voice, I knew I wanted to work with a spiritual mentor to help guide me to my next way of working. When a friend introduced me to Julie Anne Hart, I knew the time was right and her channelling was like no other I had experienced before. She was the translator of the ancient wisdoms that were held in my soul. Through our work together, I developed Embody Your Essence with the Energetic Self Success System. It's a beautiful practice that blends acupressure points with guided meditation and the breath; a self-practice, based on the ancient wisdoms, that, when practised regularly, helps bring you back into your body in the most calm and centring of ways. Finally, a way in which to reclaim the scattered parts of your body mind spirit to create a sense of peace and wholeness.

Embody your Essence with the Energetic Self Success System follows 12 pathways, each pathway building up the previous one until we reach complete Activation and Advancement on Pathway 12, whereby we connect with the Heaven and Earth within and the Circle of Life around us and we become one. Each pathway sets the intention for how it will support our body's energetic system and bring us back in to wholeness. I thought it would be helpful to share each of these pathways with you to bring you back to your wholeness. I invite you to feel into them and notice how your body responds to the words.

As you do so, ask yourself this question:

•    How is my body receiving the information?

Bring your awareness into your body. Imagine your breath flowing down the front of your body and into your belly. Focus your attention in the space in your lower belly and connect with the energy and wisdom you hold deep within you. Come out of your head and into your body, allowing the energy to soak down into your belly and connecting with the wisdom deep within you.

**Intention for Pathway 1 - Cleanse**

The energy pathways on and in our bodies play a huge part in the balance and the overall wellbeing of our systems: body, mind and spirit. When we are connected and have a sense of our Qi (our energy/life force), we are able to influence our health and vitality in the most beautiful way.

There are many different challenges put upon our systems in the modern day: from what we eat, how we move, the sheer overload of information we consume and how we live and work. The further away from nature and its rhythms and cycles we live, the harder our bodies have to work to maintain some semblance of balance.

To begin with, we need to start to notice and pay attention to our body/energy system, which absorbs so much every day on our behalf, without our asking or acknowledgement. We are opening up communication with our body so we can learn how to unblock, move, soothe and maintain our energy, creating resilience and learning the wisdom that is held within our physical being.

As with any system, our bodies work best when the energy is clean and the pathways are clear. It is fitting, then, that we start with cleansing the system within the First Pathway of the Energetic Self Success System. Think of it as emptying out the bathwater, so that we may begin to clean the bath, refresh and refill it with warm soothing cleansing water that touches the soul.

Cleansing of our energy pathways regularly supports a more efficient body, mind and spirit. The more often you can practise Pathway 1, the more you will be supporting your system and creating a whole new level of performance. This in turn helps us to be more inspired and intuitive without diminishing or depleting ourselves.

In this pathway we are connecting with the liver and gall bladder pathways, which are our natural cleansers. We are filtering out the unwanted detritus that silts up our system and letting it go, clearing and cleansing the energy highways and byways and preparing the way for what we are next going to ask our energy to do.

**Intention for Pathway 2 - Flow**

The second pathway is about creating flow in our energy system. We need to turn on the tap to clean the residue, letting the water flow throughout the system without a plug to block the flow. As we do this, we widen the energy channels, bringing clarity and a higher level of awareness.

We are starting to awaken the energy system, encouraging, widening and strengthening the flow around the body and clearing remaining obstructions.

We use sweeping and free-flowing movements, connecting the left and right sides of our body and beginning to bring everything into balance. We are strengthening the energy flow from the base of the spine right up to the top of the head, connecting heaven and earth through our body, linking in the whole of the nervous system, clearing the mind and feeding our senses.

We pay particular attention to connecting into the belly/abdomen, as this is where we often disconnect from our body, and so we begin to strengthen the base, which supports us and holds us upright.

Pathway 2 begins with the lightest of touch, brushing our energy and gently inviting it to move. We are learning how to listen to what our energy system is whispering to us and to dance with our energy as it expands and connects internally and externally.

## Intention for Pathway 3 - Pattern

To complete the first quarter of the 12 Pathway sequence, we follow Cleanse and Flow with a moment of reflection. Once the energy is cleansed and in flow, we are able to re-set the pattern within our system. We are now ready to interrupt old and unhelpful patterns that no longer serve, to re-interpret and dissolve them away and to welcome changes that are woven anew from our own DNA. We hold important wisdom in our DNA; our energy pathways weave and cross over in a knitted pattern of knowledge, experience, thoughts and feelings.

With the movement in Pathway 3, we connect with our brainwaves through our hands and weave a new pattern that will multiply our desires and create success as we hear ourselves speaking our new vision. We are safely anchored in our body and able to let go with kindness unhelpful thoughts, feelings and experiences that become stuck on repeat in our body's energy system. We are interrupting the old ways by consciously choosing to introduce a new pattern of being to our system. This is where we choose how we want to show up and create in the world. We are focusing on our best vision of and for ourselves. As you pause for reflection, you may choose to silently send your request to the divine spirit for a new way of being, asking for help and allowing your new pattern to form. Share your affirmations with the divine spirit. Feel, sense, see and know that your new way of being is forming.

## Intention for Pathway 4 - Power

It's time to power up from the Earth, to apply the energy of the Earth's system into your own. The Earth is an inexhaustible source of inspiration, innovation and creativity. Earth energy ignites and accelerates health and wellbeing. All the elements feed the Earth and charge her up: the stars, the moon, the rain, wind and sun. Connecting with the Earth and our energy accelerates and activates flow in our body, which in turn activates the mind.

The pathways in our feet are the source of much power. Energy comes up from the feet, upwards through the body, into the torso, and to the top of the head, connecting to the heavens. In this pathway we are activating the kidney meridian through the feet, connecting with our energy essence, powering up and activating our own energy system. Working on both sides of both ankles, we are balancing the yin and yang, male and female aspects of our energy, promoting harmony, symmetry and flow.

As you do this work it will create a natural feeling of being replenished, calming anxiety and releasing cortisol. Our symptomatic system (signs of dis-ease) is often caused by disconnection in our energetic system. We look at symptoms as needing a cure. In the Energetic Self Success System, when we connect and interlink with each pathway, we can release energies and move into alignment with our own unique pathways. When our pathways are opened and aligned, we have the power to create.

Take time if you can to go outside, barefoot in the Earth, sea and sand. Honour your breath and feel your energies merge with the Earth through the soles of your feet.

## Intention for Pathway 5 - Peace

When we are at peace within our body, we are in balance and at optimum health.

If we see our emotions as energy in motion, we fuel our energy systems with the emotions we have within. When we pour in emotions such as fear, worry and anger, this can block our system, creating a complete breakdown over time. When we are fuelled with the power of peace, we create a beautiful energy vault of 5-star fuel that runs our system at maximum efficiency and effectiveness.

When we invite peace into our body, we are also connecting peacefully with our spirit. To do this we need to connect into our belly, as that is where the true source of our unique life force resides. The belly holds the wisdom, the deep knowing. When we connect with our belly in peace we make clearer decisions, with greater compassion and kindness.

Our emotions sit in our solar plexus, but sometimes unpleasant emotions get stuck and then sink into our belly. At this point, we often disconnect from our belly area because, naturally, we don't like to feel those unpleasant feelings. Breathing peace into our belly is about gentle re-connection with the source of our spirit. We can have peace in our heart but if we want the whole body *knowing* and connection to the core of ourselves and the greatest well of creativity, we need to connect peacefully to the whole of our system, including the belly.

## Intention for Pathway 6 - Perception

Minds perceive, bellies conceive. As humans, we most often rely on the mind, our thoughts and perceptions, to determine what we see as the truth. But our human mind is limited, as we use our eyes to perceive but our eyes are governed by the pattern of the mind, which seldom associates with the truth but more with our interpretation of the situation. We see from within our head, seeing what we think, all an illusion and delusion of our own limited imagination. When we imagine our vision of the future from this limited place, we are cutting ourselves off from all the limitless possibilities the Universe has to offer and the deep wisdom that we hold within our DNA.

Deep connection to self allows the truth to be seen in all things. When we tune into our third eye – the seat of our true vision – and use our connection to the belly/base – where our deep knowing and unlimited creativity lies – *then* we are able to change the way we see and allow our dreams to flow into fruition. In this pathway, we are connecting into our body with faith and trust, welcoming in all the possibilities that the Universe has to offer and letting go of the limitations we have imagined for ourselves in the past.

**Intention for Pathway 7 - The Sacred Pathway**

In the second half of the Energetic Self Success System, Pathways 7 to 12, we are moving to and activating a higher consciousness, igniting pathways that have not been open until now. We are connecting with our ancestral wisdom and innate knowledge, which is locked in our DNA, awakening and accessing the magnificence that lies within. When we align with the 7th pathway, we begin to see and sense so much more; we connect with our inner wisdom, integrating it with the knowledge from our ancestors.

As we engage with the area around the belly button we connect with the umbilicus, where your spirit enters at birth, the connection to life force and deep knowing. We have gently begun to connect with this area in previous pathways, but now we're going deeper. You are more than the sum of your experiences in this lifetime, and we are celebrating the miracle of your existence, your unique and sacred energy, the journey of your soul. You, and we, are being honoured at all levels in this moment.

**Intention for Pathway 8 - Infinite Knowledge**

The human spirit is *infinite* and eternal, filled with limitless, undefinable potential, power and prosperity. We are always moving into more.

Knowledge is made up of two parts – *know* and ledge.

*Knowing* something is about what you have walked, learned and experienced. Emotions have to be activated to *know* something; you cannot know if you cannot feel. Knowing is felt deep in the body and has nothing to do with the intellect (told to you) of the mind.

*Ledge* is the ledger or the log. The ledger of you is written on your soul. The knowledge of what is imprinted on your soul is the wisdom.

The actions in Pathway 8 connect us to all the senses and sources of Infinite Knowledge:

- to the Yin Tang/ third eye which connects us to the heavenly energy all around us, to the spirit of the thought where we can receive light, expand and stretch the mind and achieve clarity;
- to the gut knowledge held in the belly, the deep, undoubtable, knowing within; and
- to the sacral area which connects us and grounds us through the base to the infinite wisdom of our Earth star.

We are connecting Heaven and Earth through our body and accessing the Infinite Knowledge without and within.

When our senses are connected, we become activated, receptive to thoughts beyond the senses to the Infinite Knowledge within our muscles, bones, blood and soul. This is a commitment to oneself, not a one-time thing but an infinite way. A consistent commitment to retreat, introspection and awareness. Success comes from one's own knowing and connection with the spirit. Expect fulfilment, the understanding of the wisdom within you.

### Intention for Pathway 9 - Movement

Any pathway is seldom straight. Even when we perceive it as straight it will bend, rise and fall in different directions. The pathway of life is often misunderstood, and Pathway 9 is about trust and surrender to life's pathway, the grace to walk the path, even when you can't see the direction of travel.

We are connecting in with the heart and lungs, which are associated with self-respect and self-love. We are honouring our own pathway, allowing us to move freely through the events that happen in our lives.

The opening of the heart allows us to understand and accept the movement of life and the infinite knowledge it has gifted us. Being open to movement gifts us the ability to receive this knowledge with grace.

The opening of the lungs is the breath: being completely in the moment, surrendering control, letting go of outcomes, releasing conditions and being in the rhythm of our own infinite knowledge.

We are learning to listen to the movement within, to see, think, be and experience differently. You sense and feel the movement and move beyond your current understanding, waking up to yourself, your potential, your infinite knowledge. Each step on the pathway of life, when understood in the context of advancing the infinite knowledge within, is welcomed. We are happy to walk the pathway, irrespective of the terrain.

## Intention for Pathway 10 - Sustaining the New Way through Source Connection

It is time for deep reflection, for we must honour our own commitment to the creation of a new way. We are here to sustain the initiation, a rite of passage into a new way of being.

We have learned that the body is a map, and we are becoming aware of which points of ignition we need to switch on in order to create a deeper connection with self. Commitment to regular implementation of the points will help sustain the new way. Now we are opening up new channels of communication to give us access to even more help and support.

Pathway 10 shows us how to move once more to a higher spiritual way, to a deeper connection to the source of self, the source of all things infinite and divine. We are stepping closer to a new way of connecting to Spirit with accountability and responsibility. A homecoming to the deeper self.

We are learning how to ask our higher self to teach us what we need to know and to learn to hear the communication from all our senses and systems. We are learning to listen to and speak from a new place that is uncontaminated by our human wants, needs and emotions. As we continuously learn to communicate with and honour our higher self, we will naturally continue to walk in a new way of being as we are sustained without and within.

## Intention for Pathway 11 - Serenity

Serenity's energy is a place of being and exists in the present moment – without having to think or do, when you are happy being where you are at, only ever in the moment, in unconditional love and acceptance.

Earth-based energy is always fully present in the power of the moment. When the feet are actively connected to Mother Earth, in a place of serenity, we are released from stress, striving and struggle.

Success comes from your knowing, becoming spontaneously more serene with a deep Earth connection, compassion for self and congruent with where you are. Serenity is the space we reside in when we are connected to self and the success occurs when everything within you is given to you. Being in this energy is the indicator that you are connected to the creation of yourself.

In placing hands to feet, we are making a beautiful connection through the body, creating unity with self. Heaven and Earth are connected and all parts are equal, in perfect balance and harmony.

As we breathe kindness and compassion into our abdomen, we deepen the connection, bringing in the unconditional love of self, sustaining serenity in a new way of understanding and self-surrender.

## Intention for Pathway 12 - Complete Activation and Advancement

Prosperity on an inner level is the key to creating and embracing prosperity on the outer level. The Energetic Self Success System's step-by-step programme is bringing you to this moment where your inner energetic circuit is complete and in balance; to an understanding that we are complete and whole beings within ourselves and in infinite connection with the energy all around us.

In this step, all 12 pathways are ignited into a circuit. Our energy is activated, aligned, balanced and charged and will therefore continue to energise us, day by day.

The pyramid is an ancient symbol for the gateway to new pathways – a powerful alignment connecting Heaven and Earth, a monument to the ascension of the spirit.

Like the pyramid, the double helix, which represents our own DNA, is also linking Earth to Heaven, rising up through the Earth, right through the core of our being, connecting into the heavens and returning back in a beautiful circuit of life.

The sun and moon bring balance and harmony to our alignment, representing the complementary aspects of masculine and feminine, yin and yang, the ebb and flow of life.

We are moving into a space where we have no compulsion to be, do or have more. We need not compare, judge or be in competition with ourselves or others because we know we are as insignificant as a speck of stardust and yet the most incredibly powerful being of honour, beauty, peace, love, serenity and deep inner knowing.

Embody your Essence with the Energetic Self Success System has been developed from a place of true love, nurtured and birthed into being with care and attention from many women. The power and infinite resource that resides within is nourished and held when we lovingly come back into connection with our body, mind and spirit. There are, of course, many practices and many paths we take as we journey through life. The invitation is always that we move and flow with the seasons and, ultimately, return home to within.

*...and so, she took a breath that went deep, deep into her belly, and knew she was home...*

# CHAPTER 8

# Resilience is Movement by Jacqueline Moore

IF YOU CAN PERCEIVE YOUR life as a movement, with experiences that are not fixed but fluid, you will begin to understand how to flow and not get stuck in feelings, spaces and relationships that are toxic, depleting and don't allow you to experience your full potential. Resilience, like life, is a movement, a way of adapting and emerging stronger and wiser than before.

Walking along the beach with my dear friend, I told her I had been asked to write about resilience but wasn't sure what to say. She turned to face me and very firmly said, "Of all the people I know, you should talk about it. Look what you have been through!"

I ran a fast forward reel in my head of some of the experiences in my life, from childhood bullying and a challenging relationship with my parents to my love of dance and the power it had to transform me and take me out of my present to a new reality, which I now understand to be a spiritual connection.

I ran away from home and was homeless and confused, rejected, alone – and then groomed, used, abused and raped by people I trusted or people who just understood that they could! I remembered the people who entered my life and saw my light and encouraged me to work, travel and study. My teachers, healers and mentors. The compassion of the martial arts community, who allowed a very mixed up and confused young woman to live and learn with them.

The joy of motherhood and the toughness of single parenthood. The wonderful experiences in my career in domestic abuse and the many strong and brave women I met. The opportunity I found during my menopause for newfound wellbeing and the conception of a new role for myself as an artist and movement coach. "Yes, okay," I said. "I can do that. I can talk about resilience."

My story, told simply, is about learning to overcome abuse, heal and develop myself as a human being.

I am a Transformational Movement Coach. For me, movement means connection to the divine, to universal energy, a spiritual connection that advances, heals, illuminates and transforms. This can be through wild movement, free expression without trained form that unlocks primal energy, creation, healing and transformation. Or by channelling movement through sacred choreography, expressing personal wisdom and potential through unique and personalised form. Or the energy medicine, science and humanity within my martial arts practice.

My vision is to make a difference in the lives of the people I work with, whatever movement form I teach.

We all have a story, we are all connected, we are all spiritual beings and we are all on the move.

All life is movement; mind, body and spiritual thoughts, decisions and actions are all sacred, and all have energy and vibration, cause and effect. Individually and collectively, we are all moving and exchanging universal energy.

When you are connected to universal energy, in whatever is your way of perceiving this – God, Great

Spirit, the Divine, goodness, magic, or great mystery – you will be centred in the energy of love and compassion, and this will inform your actions. Our challenge is to remain in this connection, so our actions or movements will be informed by love. However, life is not so simple. We are all negotiating so many relationships, responsibilities and obligations in our daily lives. Our need for resilience is clear.

Our minds are often dwelling in the past or concerned about the future and stressed in the present.

As we negotiate our daily lives, new circumstances can trigger old wounds, moving us into stress, conflict, denial, apathy or burnout. Our future path becomes a hard road to follow and not an unfolding pathway full of intrigue, joy, curiosity, opportunity and personal growth.

As a movement coach, I can see the results of stress, trauma and hardship in the body as it may translate into mental and physical ill health. It may transpire as burnout, stagnation, inflexibility, limited movement, constricted flow and pain. When beautiful souls (and we all are) do not see their own beauty, it is a great shame. Universal energy is always waiting for us to connect, to support and encourage us to shine, equally ready to catch us and nurture us when we need it.

The benefits of exercise do not need explaining, especially in hard and challenging times where we need to be resilient, to bounce back and emerge stronger than before.

There is a deeper meaning and potential to developing resilience through movement beyond exercise. Moving with an awareness of what is happening in the body physically, emotionally, and spiritually. Connecting to universal energy through movement and maintaining and developing this connection as often as possible. Using this connection to heal, inform and direct all the movements in your life, distinguishing life itself as movement from birth to death.

My martial arts training taught me the potential in movement to develop resilience through self-awareness, acceptance, respect and discipline. You do not have to train as a martial artist, but you may use the philosophy behind martial arts movements to inform your approach to life.

A martial artist understands that there are no mistakes, only experiences. Experiences can be extremely painful or pleasurable and everything in between those two spectra; nevertheless, they are all simply experiences and will pass. Life is movement. Our aim is to stay balanced and to flow internally and externally with universal energy.

One of the first things I learnt in my martial arts training was to fall on all kinds of surfaces, no mats. We trained without mats so we could learn how to fall and land without fear or injury. This meant to be aware, accept and stay balanced throughout the fall and the landing.

In life, when hard experiences occur there is nothing between us and them, no cushions or mats; there is just the experience: how it feels, the fall and the landing, then the rising up and the moving forward. Learning to fall conquers the fear of falling. It also teaches, at its core, to accept and be aware of what is happening now, in the past and in the future without fear. Without acceptance and awareness there is always fear – and where there is fear there is conflict.

We all fall, off track, course, plan and path, then beat ourselves up, feeling guilt, shame and inner conflict. Or we receive a 'hit', a blow of some kind, a force or action from a person, persons, or circumstances that throws us. We feel hurt, shocked, overwhelmed, resentful, angry, fearful, worried or humiliated. We are literally floored!

When you learn to fall without fear, you learn to feel, be aware and accept, to fall gracefully in flow with universal energy, land safely and with awareness, rise and move on. This is resilience in emotion and motion.

Without awareness (feeling) and acceptance (falling), we get stuck in conflict and fear, where we can become a victim or a tyrant to ourselves or others.

To build resilience, we must be honest and aware of how we feel and accept the experience. It doesn't matter if we fall, because if we are aware and accept, we stay connected to universal energy. This means we do not lose our balance, we retain our self-love, we have the opportunity to grow and be shaped positively by the experience. When we disconnect from universal energy, we lose the opportunity to be supported. To stay connected in challenging times gives us the power of resilience to land safely and leverage up and recreate ourselves and our circumstances with self-discipline.

Getting stuck in negative feelings and energy is extremely harmful to our health and wellbeing. It is not truly being honest about who we are and acknowledging our potential.

Developing resilient skills will empower you to emerge stronger than before. Grow as a human being and improve your quality of life. This takes self-discipline, numerous actions of self- respect, love, and care. This is resilience in action. These acts can be as simple as preparing healthy and nutritious foods, drinking water, taking time out to run a bath, walking in nature, reading a book, learning to meditate, or more profound, like booking a weekend retreat or investing in a coach or mentor. These actions collectively form a movement, and this movement is our resilience.

Our actions of self-discipline will be determined by our circumstances. As a domestic abuse worker, I often asked women to list the ways in which they could show love to their children. Often the reaction in the group was joyful with the realisation that their lists of actions did not cost money and therefore were entirely possible to them.

The concept of self-discipline may be intimidating because it implies the need for will power and nerves of steel. Often it is our perceived lack of willpower that crushes our ability to push through in those times when we need resilience, leaving us feeling depressed, guilty and ashamed.

Don't forget when you are connected to universal energy, therefore self-love and compassion, there is no room for guilt and shame. How do you feel when you do the things that give you pleasure, that make your heart sing? When you create something with your skills, spend time with your beloveds, walk in beautiful surroundings, listen to a piece of music that expresses exactly how you feel? These are acts of self-love and therefore connect you to universal energy. Self-discipline is an act of self-love, self-respect and deepest self-care. Play with the letters and you will find the word 'disciple'.

A disciple follows a spiritual path with dedication, love and faith. Becoming a disciple of your own wellbeing and self-love means a dedication and faith in you and your connection to your spiritual path, your relationship with the divine, your flow with universal energy, your purpose and potential.

Create a list of actions you can take, at least a hundred, from the simplest to the more determined, that include your mind, body and spirit. Use the power of self-discipline to be a disciple of your own self-love, care and potential and do them with love and appreciation for yourself. Here are some ideas to get you started.

| | | |
|---|---|---|
| o Walk in nature | o Read | o Visit an ancient place |
| o Kick into the wind | o Find new authors | o Buy essential oils |
| o Stand barefoot on the earth | o Be creative | o Healthy foods |
| o Breathe deeply | o Get up earlier | o Collect feathers |
| o Candle gaze | o Dance | o Prepare special meals |
| o Learn to meditate | o Invest in yourself | o Stretch your muscles |
| o Paint your toes | o Sing in the shower | o Treat yourself |
| o Soak your feet | o Connect with friends | o Hug and kiss |
| o Give yourself a massage | o Retreat for a day | o Fresh flowers |
| o | o | o |
| o | o | o |
| o | o | o |
| o | o | o |

Keep growing your list. Keep your list close by so you can do them when you need to transform your energy. It will feel challenging at times, but resilience is movement, a pushing through, a doing of self-love.

A martial artist may learn how to fight but will use their awareness to avoid spaces and places of conflict and fight only when they absolutely have to – and then do as little harm as possible. Being honest also means blocking, punching and throwing when you need to. You cannot let something throw you ruthlessly and relentlessly and continue to engage in the movement. Your only act of final resilience may be to say 'NO'. By saying no, you honour yourself. It is a powerful act of self- love and self -respect. Saying no is a change of response, a new tactic, the application of a new way of behaving.

You can say no to a form of negative behaviour and energy that is directed towards you. A relationship that is no longer healthy and is depleting you. A job that burns you out and has become unfulfilling. Creation in your business that is not in alignment with your values. A pattern of behaviour or a habit that does not nourish you.

Remember the wisdom in falling: be aware, feel, accept, allow yourself to fall without injury and without fear, and rise and say no without fear or conflict. You will find a new way through your connection with universal energy, the acts of self-love.

In order to open up the space for new beginnings and new experiences, you have to let go of those things that harm or no longer serve you. Sometimes that is very straightforward. Other times it is more painful or complicated; it may even be impossible. However, there is always room for forward movement and transformation in any situation.

I have a wonderful client, a talented artist, kind, compassionate, and intelligent. She is a mother and carer of two incredible special needs children who are extremely talented, energetic and very exhausting. She cannot say no to this situation, but she is able to use her resilience through her martial arts practice in order to continue to thrive within her situation. Practising her movements means she is able to connect and maintain a connection with universal energy from deep within her that radiates out into her home, garden and beyond. The movements have helped her to heal her body and reduce pain and inflammation.

She is able to replenish her energy when she needs to and not allow trauma to enter her body; to feel, accept and release negative emotions as they arise in the moment. She keeps her joints juicy and flexible, her muscles strong and her posture balanced. Her organs function harmoniously together and do not get stuck and sluggish because she is in conflict with her daily life.

She embodies the meanings behind the movements to become more aware, feel, accept, and create a vision for her future that is attainable. Therefore, when she opens the wings of the crane, she is open to the possibilities in life and releases the obstacles that stop her creative expression. When she punches, she breathes life into her projects. When she practises the angel looking in the mirror, she sees her reflection and appreciates who she is.

She has used her list of actions of self-discipline to nurture herself and create boundaries and time for her own wellbeing. She is happier, healthier and feeling positive about her future. She is an inspiration and a magnificent example of the power in movement and resilience in action.

When you see life as a movement that always has the potential for connection to universal energy, you will become more resilient because you will understand that experiences are fluid and moving. You will accept falling or being thrown without fear as transitory and rise again with a deeper understanding of yourself and others.

You will understand that self-discipline is self-love, self-care and self-respect in action and create abundant ways of showing this to yourself. You will recognise that there are times when you need to say no without compromise. Accept when you cannot but still create abundant ways of giving yourself self-love, self-care and self-respect. This is resilience in movement. You will not get stuck; you will move on.

# CHAPTER 9

# Finding Food Freedom by Lucy West

LIKE ME, MANY WOMEN WILL have spent most of their lives consumed by self-obsession over their bodies, dieting rules, in constant stress and worry about food and weight. You might be one of them.

My hope is that in this chapter you can find relief, healing and freedom around this topic. To be free from guilt, fear and worry and truly return to yourself and allow yourself the nourishing relationship with food that it should be. You deserve that freedom.

If you are anything like me, you would have grown up with many influences and beliefs around food. So, let's dive in...

How old were you when you first heard your mother talking about diets?

I was probably just six or seven, but I may have been younger. My mother did not need to diet. She was a very active, healthy young woman and was certainly not overweight.

I also remember my grandmother giving me a Rosemary Conley diet book around the age of 14. What are your earliest memories?

On a completely subconscious level, we have inherited beliefs, habits and behaviours from our parents on many things – and our relationship with food is one of them.

I remember deciding to become a vegetarian at just six years old, scraping the bits of meat from the plate of my school dinner and throwing them under the table, only to be told off by the dinner ladies.

My main reason for the decision was because my mother was a vegetarian and at that young age, I simply wanted to model her behaviour.

Back to childhood experiences surrounding food. For us, money was in very limited supply. My father worked, my mother didn't. Dinners were simple: fish fingers, peas and a few potatoes type thing. Dessert might be a packet of Angel Delight between us. My brother and I were on free school meals because we were a low-income family, which meant we had to eat whatever was dished out at school. I used to be so envious of the kids with their lunch boxes, with all their packaged snacks and processed food.

We ate well. I never remember being hungry. We never ate out but we weren't really aware that it was a thing. The most exciting it might get would be going to McDonald's for a friend's birthday party.

My brother and I would get so excited about visiting our Granny Gerry, as she would cook for the whole family from her tiny little council house kitchen. She would serve us the most delicious and, more importantly, huge roast dinner you've ever seen. Her plates were those oval blue and white Victorian type plates that she would fill to the brim. We would be so full we often had to go and lie down on her squishy bed after eating. An hour or so later she would offer us cheese and ham sandwiches on that fluffy white bread you only got from a bakery – not to mention her special sweet jar, from which she would let my brother and me choose some goodies.

This was a luxury for us, as we never had these types of 'treats' at home – so perhaps this is where my first beliefs around 'treats' and 'naughty food' came from.

I never thought much about my weight, growing up. I was a pretty average, healthy-looking child; not chubby, and not skinny. We were active kids who always played outdoors after school. I took dance lessons a few times a week and our weekend family activities usually involved long walks.

That was until my teens. I'd made a decision pretty early on in life that I wanted to pursue a career as an actress, dancing and singing on the West End stage. I dreamt of going to stage school in London and pursuing a theatre career or even joining a girl band.

Like most teenage girls in the 90s, I was a true fan and follower of The Spice Girls, later closely following their solo careers. Geri Halliwell became famous for her epic body transformation, which she credited to daily yoga. Naturally, when she released her yoga VHS I bought it and followed.

In 2001, a magazine was published called Celebrity Bodies, similar in format to Heat but only focused on the subject of the title, with headlines such as Dimpled Thigh Alert – how to beat cellulite the celebrity way or New Star Diets for your Dream Body.

This was like the Holy Grail for me to follow. At the tender age of 15, and wanting to pursue my dream of becoming a pop star, I now had a bible to follow.

It basically went like this; eat salad, more salad and a bit of brown rice = size 0 figure.

So that is what I did.

I was not aware that Geri's tiny physique was actually the result of an eating disorder. I thought it was perfectly healthy to live off zero breakfast, a lunch of brown rice and raw peppers and a small evening meal. All the while, I was very active at dance classes most nights.

I definitely experimented with the idea of bulimia. Again, it seemed like a lot of celebrities were staying skinny that way but after a few attempts of making myself sick I decided I would really rather eat small meals and feel hungry all day.

Discipline and punishment were my middle names. All my friends were amazed that I could eat so little and I kind of wore it as a badge of honour. I still felt too fat but, in reality, I was very slim and most likely underweight for my age and height.

Reflecting back on this gruelling time, it is now clear how entwined my relationship with food was to the emotions I was feeling at that time. I was so ready to break free and escape the small town I'd grown up in, desperate to pursue something new and exciting. Not to mention the GCSE exam stress and pressure. My periods stopped completely and I even developed skin problems, getting psoriasis all down my arms and legs.

My dreams came true when I was accepted to study musical theatre at The BRIT School, a performing arts college in London for 14-18-year-olds, which was completely subsided so you could attend for free.

Therefore, at the tender age of 16, I left sleepy Suffolk and made my way to The Big Smoke. I was happier, freer, and loving life at stage school and I didn't punish myself in the same way. I ate what I wanted and felt pretty confident, although infinitely aware I was not one of the skinny dancer types in my year group. My thighs definitely touched – not cool in ballet class.

It's crazy to me now that during my time at stage school, when we were on our feet for eight hours a day, we were not taught about the importance of nutrition and food. We were simply left to it. I hope this has changed now, although I have heard horror stories from friends who went on to further dance colleges being told to lose weight or they would be kicked out.

This was a time of real freedom and happiness for me. I probably didn't eat particularly well and certainly had discovered alcohol and partying! But I was physically active – dancing for hours, walking miles as I didn't have a car, rushing from job to job. My twenties followed a similar pattern and I never really considered my eating habits, nutrition and health relating to food until I started my online wellness business when I was 27.

Well, this was a complete revelation for me:

*Food is fuel*
*You are what you eat*
*Food is the cause of disease*

This information blew my mind and it's taken years of learning, trial and error to understand what works for me, so I hope the following information will be beneficial to you as you read it.

Now, well into in my thirties, I have learned what food types, patterns and habits serve me and what don't.

That doesn't mean anything is off the table.

I still love pizza, wine and chocolate. I just know having those things all the time does not make me feel amazing or in my highest alignment.

Every piece of food has a vibrational energy. Highly processed food, full of sugar and preservatives, is very low in its vibration. You might feel the initial 'hit' from eating it but soon after you will crash. You will either need to go with that crash and ride it out OR you keep going with more sugary snacks to keep that false 'high'. If this is your pattern, you will tend to wake up feeling lethargic, groggy and demotivated.

Alternatively, if you consume high vibration foods such as lots of leafy greens, whole foods such as lentils, good proteins, and healthy fats you will feel full, satiated and you will notice you have energy and stamina throughout the day, not just that quick hit and burn out.

The reason behind this is the connection to our gut health. Everything we consume has to be processed through the gut and certain foods are easier work for the gut to digest than others.

In fact, our gut bacteria regulates many of our bodily functions, from creating vitamins to controlling our immune system, brain function and of course, metabolism and weight. What happens in our gut is critical to our long-term health.

*"Many of us have too few bacteria in our intestines, where they do us the most good. Others have an overgrowth of the bad kind, which causes its own problems. Not enough of the good bacteria, or too much of the bad, can lead to intestinal disorders like Irritable Bowel Syndrome, Leaky Gut, and SIBO, but also chronic inflammation, depression, even cancer and heart disease." - Dr Mark Hyman*

## NUTRITION FUNDAMENTALS

OK, so what are the fundamental parts of nutrition to focus on in order to save this distorted connection to our bodies?

These are my thoughts, based on many hours of reading, watching and listening to experts on the subject but most importantly from learning through my own personal experience. Awareness is key and the starting point to change. This is going to be a lifelong healing journey, which you can take one step at a time. View it with excitement, curiosity and fun. Have a playful attitude towards it. It should not feel gruelling or punishing.

As I have already explained, there is no strict rule book of what you can or cannot eat. Every human is different and what works for me may not work for you. However, let's talk about different nutrients and start to observe what is serving us and what doesn't.

**Refined Sugar** – As you probably already know, sugar is highly addictive and problematic if we have too much. This is because it has been stripped of all nutrients, draining and leaching the body of precious vitamins and minerals. In an attempt to remove excess sugar from our blood stream we produce a hormone called insulin, which is also known as our fat storing hormone, as it helps convert the sugar into fatty acids which are then stored in the most inactive areas of our bodies. As we consume more and more sugar, we produce more and more insulin and eventually our cells become deaf to the insulin, leading to insulin resistance. This is the beginning of type II diabetes. Sugar is hidden in many different foods, especially table sauces and breads, so do become aware of how much you are really consuming. Not only will you avoid excess weight gain from not over consuming sugar, you will avoid the huge energy slumps that come post consumption too.

**Dairy** – Despite the widespread notion that dairy is healthy, consuming pasteurised dairy is frequently associated with a decline in health. Many people lose the enzyme that digests dairy after the age of two and it is estimated that a whopping 70% of the world's population is intolerant to dairy. Once raw milk is pasteurised, only around 30% of the calcium in a glass of milk actually gets absorbed. You will obtain twice as much calcium from a cup of broccoli. Many leafy green vegetables are loaded with calcium and magnesium too. If you are going to have dairy milk, opt for a raw unpasteurised one (unless you're pregnant) and find a reputable farm that feeds its cattle on grass and is organic.

**Gluten** – Gluten is a family of proteins found in grains. They are thick and make things stick together when baked instead of falling apart. It is estimated that 50% of the population has difficulty breaking down gluten in their intestines. When the immune system recognises gluten as a 'foreign protein' it attacks and damages the intestinal wall, leading to swelling on the intestines (pot belly/bloating). Over time, the intestinal wall can become so thin and damaged that small holes appear. This is known as leaky gut, and results in an array of problems as undigested proteins can enter the blood stream.

I really love my carbs and all my nearest and dearest know this about me. I would take a round of toast over some chocolate any day. I will never give up bread, pasta or pizza as I love it all. However, what I've learned on my journey is that too much gluten or carbs makes me feel very tired and sluggish, to the point where I've often had to take a nap afterwards.

Therefore, I may enjoy gluten at dinner time, after I've finished my workday or a pizza on a Saturday night. I just know that I will most likely feel pretty slow and even slightly hungover afterwards. Would I want to eat that first thing in the morning or the night before an important speaking event in my business? Probably not!

I used to love porridge for breakfast, but I noticed I would feel sleepy and bloated after having it and hungry by 11am. Now I have a smoothie including some vegan protein powder and I feel AMAZING. I feel satisfied, full – but not that tummy bloating type of full – and I am fuelled right until lunch time. However, my husband LOVES oats in the morning and they make him feel great! It really is about tuning in to your body and seeing what you react best to.

**Fats** – Fats don't make you fat! This is old outdated advice from the late 80s. Thinking fat makes you fat is like thinking blueberries make you blue!! Think about that for a moment.

Fat actually helps your body function, your metabolism to run properly and your hormones to be in balance which plays a HUGE role in weight management and your brain function.

It is excess sugar and high carbohydrate diets that cause weight gain and damage to the arteries and heart.

As you can see, we need saturated fat and omega 3 fatty acids so much. We need cholesterol too. Therefore, all those fats that have been touted as baddies: give them a chance!

Fats that should be avoided are rancid fats that have been in plastic containers in daylight, and trans fats, which are abundant in pre-packaged foods. Vegetable oils are also a problem as we have them in excess ,which increases inflammation in the body.

Here is a list of the good fats to have:

- Coconut oil (this is a WONDER food!)
- Avocado
- Nuts and seeds
- Cold pressed olive oil, avocado oil, macadamia oil
- Animal fats from organic grass-fed animals
- Olives
- Oily fish

Not only that, fat makes food taste GOOD!! Low fat diets are bland and loaded with carbs and artificial

flavours to make them actually taste of something –
so embrace the fats.

**Alcohol** – There is literally no nutritional benefit to
drinking alcohol, so why do we do it?

- It de-stresses us
- It's sociable
- It's fun
- It's relaxing
- It's enjoyable

But how do you really feel after?
Do you know when you've had too much?

I started drinking and partying heavily from the
age of 14 right into my late 20s. I still absolutely LOVE
a good knees up, and that party animal spirit isn't
going anywhere.

But where I used to drink myself to the point
where I couldn't stand up or get myself into a taxi,
things have very much changed. I'm squiffy after two
wines and I guess, because of everything I have
explained thus far in this chapter, I just know when
my body has had enough and says NO THANK YOU
to any more. I'm quite happy dancing the night away
for the rest of the night with a bottle of water.

Like everything I've written so far, it's about being mindful. Alcohol is a drug and it will lower your vibe and energy, particularly the next day, so just plan and consider when it's really worth having that next drink.

**Caffeine** – OK, so I'm British and we Brits love tea. This is very much a social tradition in an English household and I so remember trying to train myself to love it as a child just so I could be like the adults and join in with 'having tea'.

I then worked for many years in the entertainment industry and went from someone who couldn't bear the smell or taste of coffee to someone who drank four or five coffees a day. How did I train myself to do this? By loading it with flavoured syrups and sugar and gradually weaning those down to be able to drink the hardcore black stuff.

My health transformation really began in 2016 when I first committed to a 30-day elimination plan (excluding gluten, dairy, refined sugar and caffeine from my diet for 30 days) and a remarkable thing happened.

I came home to my younger self. I no longer wanted the coffee or the tea. It simply did not interest me. I didn't crave it and I found the smell repulsive. I felt amazing and more energised without it.

Yes, of course that first week or so off it was pretty terrible with headaches but by halfway through I didn't miss it at all. I craved herbal tea and I could really taste the different flavours of tea, whether it was peppermint, berries or fennel.

Again – nature! It has always been in our intuition to use nature's flavours and herbs to serve us. It is what our ancestors did, after all.

**Meat / Fish** – This is always a controversial one to discuss.

Here's where I am at personally. I choose not to eat meat and haven't for many years.

I once heard someone discuss eating animals as eating another living soul's fear.

When I thought about that, it cut pretty deep. As I'm sure you are beginning to learn and acknowledge on this spiritual journey, everything truly is energy and we are all connected.

I therefore made the choice that I did not want to consume the energy or vibration of fear from another living creature.

My perception also changed weirdly when I got my own animals as an adult. We had always had cats and dogs during my childhood, when I was veggie. The time I stopped being veggie was after I'd left home and no longer had animals living with me, whilst I was at college and university and then into my busy career and travelling.

Once I bought my first home and got my fur babies (two gorgeous, very spoilt rescue cats), I would look at them and look at the meat on my plate and feel awful and sad.

I would look at their little faces and think, "But how is a cow or a pig any different?" It has a heart and a soul and a personality just like them, so really, the decision to not eat meat any longer was easy.

I do not judge anyone for their food choices. If you are happy and feel good and healthy eating meat, especially if it is organic and as natural as it can be, then all good.

However, science and research continues to illuminate the benefits of a plant-based diet, not only on our bodies but in order to sustain the health of the planet we live on.

If going vegan or veggie is not for you, how about a Meat Free Monday?

You will be amazed by how creative you can get when you experiment with cooking without meat and the amazing flavours that can be enjoyed.

## Everybody is Different

It is merely our job to observe what feels good and right for us.

Please know that all the things listed are not your enemy. You can enjoy them but perhaps you will consider eating some of those things more in moderation. You can even trial an elimination programme for 30 days and see how much better your body feels and functions. This elimination programme will allow your body to take a break from some of the most common allergens.

Again, I am not here to tell you what is right or wrong or what to eat, but I hope now you are armed with this information, it can be a starting point for you to make those intuitive decisions on what foods will work for you and bring you back to your highest, most vibrant self.

## Self-Love

Let's remember that nutrition alone is not the whole conversation!!

This is so fundamental, because our emotions, thoughts, feelings, stress levels, relationships and work life all affect our eating patterns.

You could be eating the most nutritious wholesome kale salad in the world but if you are frantically shovelling it down in five minutes so you don't have to deal with that awkward situation in your relationship, is it still healthy?

You are probably familiar with the term 'emotional eating' and this is often seen as a negative thing. To be honest, I'd like to throw that perception out. I believe our emotions are with us at all times. They aren't something we should try and hide and just make them go away; that won't work. However, in terms of eating, having an awareness of our emotions before we tuck in can certainly help us in many ways.

Imagine this...you get home from a very stressful day at work and you go to reach for the crisps and dips as you feel so enraged and just need something to hit the spot right now. (No judgement – I've definitely been there many times.)

How about instead you just take five minutes to sit on your bed or sofa, put on some calming music or a guided meditation and simply BE with your breath for a few precious moments. Release some of that stress from your day and come back to your body and yourself before you dive into those snacks for comfort.

Maybe say some affirmations or mantras out loud or in your mind:

*I am worthy*
*I am safe*
*I am loved*
*I am valued*
*I allow myself grace to simply be*

Then notice how you feel. Do you still feel like going for that binge?

Or does your body say, "Please nourish me! I want a comforting soup, or a fresh crunchy stir fry." Or maybe you want pie and chips! Honestly, any of these options is OK. All I'm saying is trust and allow yourself to LISTEN to what you really need.

Our biggest worry when we let go of the rules and restrictions around food is that we don't trust ourselves. Our limited subconscious thoughts tell us we would go wild and eat crap all day every day.

But this really is not the case. Once you slow down and listen to your body, it will tell you what you need. What is in your highest good. What will make you feel amazing. What will allow you to vibrate at your highest level.

You may be convinced that you are addicted to and crave sugar, but your healthiest happiest self doesn't crave sugar, it craves vitamins and minerals and an abundant fun lifestyle full of ease, flow and grace.

My husband and I often joke about our weird broccoli craving when we have been on the road travelling. Too many days of eating low vibe foods (think lots of beige and fried things) has us feeling out of alignment and we are quickly craving those greens again! We also sometimes crave doughnuts – but hey, it's all about balance, right?

We need to end the war with our bodies and our relationship with food. What relationship have you ever had where anything was resolved with anger, bitterness or regret? Just like a relationship with another human, this relationship can be healed with communication, acceptance, listening, nurturing and massive amounts of love and forgiveness.

Quite honestly, the world we live in today is setting us up to fail. We are bombarded with information and media overload. We have distractions and notifications galore and all this factors into the disconnection in our intuitive relationship to our bodies.

When you start observing your thoughts around food rather than going through obsessive patterns and habits, you will find deep wisdom ready to be unearthed.

**Ask:**
- How do I feel before eating?
- What are my reasons for eating this?
- How do I feel after?
- In what ways do I sabotage myself?
- What can I do to support myself?
- What patterns am I noticing?

Observe those thoughts like an outsider looking in. Study yourself and your habits without judgement.

Just be curious and ASK.

Intuition, that inner guidance system, is going to become your greatest gift on this journey within. I know it's not easy but, like anything in life, the journey is worthwhile: the journey of inner wisdom and knowing and finding that sacred connection back to ourselves.

It is life changing and invaluable for your physical, mental, emotional and spiritual health to allow you to elevate to your truest, highest potential.

You deserve complete freedom in your body, you deserve boundless energy, you deserve to fall in love with your body and yourself.

Never sacrifice a healthy mindset in pursuit of a healthy body.

How many times have you punished and berated your body for being too wobbly, too scrawny, too dimpled, too pale, too anything? When was the last time you showed your body love and gratitude?

Pop your journal out for two minutes and brainstorm as many reasons as you can for why you are grateful for your body.

Here are some prompts, but allow your mind to wander and free flow:

- You birthed a child
- You ran a race
- You danced all night with friends
- You hugged your family
- You built something amazing
- You nurtured a garden
- You climbed a mountain

We only have one place to live – our bodies. Your body will always be your home, so it's time to start loving, appreciating and nourishing yourself.

The divine connection between your body and soul must be nourished and your relationship with food plays a huge role in this.

The more we binge, diet, purge and starve ourselves, the more disconnected we become.

Connect to your heart and soul before deciding what goes on your plate.

It's time we learned to love, nourish and empower our bodies.

I hope this chapter has helped you find relief and freedom around food and be truly guilt free in your food choices.

By taking the time to hone in and listen to what your body truly needs and what really fuels you, you will find freedom in food.

You can relax and enjoy those special occasions, holidays and treats whilst dropping the guilt and fear.

You are safe and capable of making wise, healthy choices and you now have the tools to get on track when life throws you off balance.

Here's to a fabulous, free and fun future.

# CHAPTER 10

# Birthing Your Brilliance by Pam Bailey

*I WAS STANDING IN THE corner of the small living room of a cottage. Sitting in a rocking chair beside the hearth of an open fire was an old woman. She was working intently on a piece of tapestry and as the only light in the room came from the roaring fire and a small candle that was burning on the table beside her, she had to hold the work up close to her eyes. All was still, save the crackling of the wood as it burnt in the hearth. I wasn't sure if she was aware of my presence, so I felt compelled to remain standing where I was, quietly observing.*

*A noise from outside made us both look up. In the split second that I realised it was a group of people, a loud hammering on the door ensued, and the old woman turned to gaze straight into my eyes.*

*The door was broken down and the room filled quickly with an army of men. Yes, they were an army: the King's Army. They were here for the old woman.*

*She didn't flinch as she was dragged to her feet but, deftly, she reached out her hand to me and I reached out to her. As she was pulled towards the door by the mob, I grasped the end thread of her needlework and the tapestry started to undo.*

*I watched quietly as the woman disappeared, tears now cascading unchecked down my face. Her eyes were eyes that I recognised. And I knew that she too recognised the eyes that had looked back at her.*

*In that moment she was me and I was her.*

*The drum changed its beat as the signal that I needed to journey back. The Shamanic meditation was finishing. Journalling my thoughts, my pen flowed. I didn't think; I just let go as the words appeared in my book. It is safe. It is safe now for women to emerge into their power. The catalysts for the level of transformative change women desire as they journey through their menopause is emerging.*

Menopause. It was a subject that was never spoken of in my family. I'm not even sure where my awareness of this event came from. But as far as I was concerned, this was something that happened when you reached your 50s; the beginning of the end of your life and old age. In the meantime, I had so much living to do.

After I left school, I started my career in the hospitality sector, qualified as a chef and met my partner. Together, we worked and travelled around the UK and abroad, until the time came for us to come back to England. We agreed that my partner would be the main bread winner going forward, so I could raise our children. In the meantime, I gave up my career as a chef and worked in a company that provided training and support to apprentices in the catering sector – on the job training. It was interesting work based locally to where we lived. As far as I was concerned, I was following the life plan I had had in my mind since I was a young girl. The next step was children, and I could leave my job, concentrate on raising them and then, when they were old enough, restart my career. I didn't have to think about getting old as I had so much to do before I got there.

I was following a path I felt was mine to follow and live. During my 31st year on Earth, my story changed and, within a few days, my world fell apart. I was made redundant on the Monday and by the Thursday of that same week, my partner came home and told me he was leaving. He moved out that same day.

I felt a failure. I was going to have to start my life over again. I was in my 30s with no job and no home, as I couldn't afford the mortgage on my own. Where previously I had made my health and wellness part of my everyday life, I was now not bothered about attending exercise classes at the gym to keep myself fit. I stopped caring about what I ate, even going through some days not eating at all. I also began to smoke, something I had experimented with in my teens but had quickly stopped. Emotionally, I was numb, but at the same time my stress levels were through the roof. I had thoughts of unworthiness and a pain in my heart centre that I had only ever experienced once before – on the death of my father.

Drifting through a haze of days that rolled from day into night, I began to have the smallest feeling of a little shaft of light wanting to make its presence known. In my dreams I got to experience a sense of standing in time whilst the world was busy moving through time, going about everyday life moving forward just as I was standing still. I knew in that moment that I would have to put my practical head back on, get a job and start life from there. And so I did, and I was extremely happy. I loved my new job, got fit, renovated a house and had a couple of relationships. Then, around my 34th or 35th birthday,

I started to get frequent migraines that sometimes lasted for two or three days and occurred three or four times a month. My friends encouraged me to see my doctor to rule out anything sinister; they were thinking brain tumours.

Never in my wildest dreams at the time did I think it was anything related to menopause. After all, that event happened when you reached your 50s, didn't it?

So, there I was, sitting in the doctor's little room, telling him all about my migraines. He asked some questions about my general health, like when I last had an eye test and what my period cycle was like. It was true that my periods had changed a bit, but I was still regular. I didn't see the connection, until he sat back in his chair and said, in a very matter of fact way, "You should expect these changes at your age." What did he mean? I was still young! What?

I responded with, "But I'm in my 30s! I have another 20 years before I have to think about getting old." I then burst into tears.

I was filled with a horror I cannot fully explain to this day, but there was an awful realisation that a door was being firmly shut in my face and I was never going to experience being a mother. It was the end of my fertility and the loss of the children I would never have. I was getting old; the last sparkling years of my life seemed to be falling away from me. What was I going to do or be?

I felt alone, old, invisible and bewildered. Why me? I hadn't known then that it was menopause, or rather the start of the phase called perimenopause. The subject was not one that had ever been discussed in my family and none of my friends were going through it; they were still having babies.

Within just a few minutes of my appointment I was back in my car, clutching a prescription for some migraine tablets. I gazed into the distance of the car park, bereft, numb, devoid of any immediate emotional response that I recognised. I was immediately struck with how alone I felt. For an event that was going to change my life forever, I had come away from the doctor's with no information leaflets or pamphlets and no further guidance from my GP about what was happening, nor what I could expect.

That night, my sleep was restless. In fact, I don't believe I slept much at all, but the next day I was so very clear on what I needed to do. This significant life change was not going to take me over! I was not going to just lie down and accept that I was now old and heading to the twilight of my years.

Growing up, I had always been taught by my mother that if I wasn't feeling particularly healthy, I should first take a look at what I was eating and drinking. I immediately stopped drinking alcohol and eating chocolate as these were two very distinct triggers for my migraines, and I started to take note of what happened to me physically and emotionally after I had eaten or taken a drink. For example, after lunch I liked to have a cup of hot tea, but that sent my hot flushes into overdrive. So, I changed it slightly and drank some water after my lunch, left it a while and then had my cup of tea. I also noticed that if I had a small snack before I went to bed, maybe a slice of melon or a couple of spoonfuls of cereal, I didn't wake up during the night with sweats. Understanding myself was key to the changes I was making and slowly, by including some specific hypnotherapy protocols and making sure I was active every day, I got myself under control again. Sure, there were times when my careful changes slipped (I am only human, after all), but I also knew without a doubt that medical intervention with HRT was never going to come into the equation. After all, menopause is a natural next phase in a woman's life and what I was experiencing was not a medical issue.

Within six months, my periods had stopped. This was it; I had no choice in the direction I was now heading. If I had been fooling myself that menopause wasn't happening and burying my emotions, the corner had been turned. I knew I was never going to be able to walk back to the woman I once was.

I changed my life plans and started on a path to running my own therapy business focusing on coaching and hypnotherapy. Freedom seemed to be the path that was beckoning me. It was calling to me loudly. Freedom so I could travel, freedom so I could choose when I worked. I was fed up with the 9 to 5 treadmill.

Eight days before my 40th birthday, I was given the opportunity to take voluntary redundancy, and I embarked on my road to self-employment. I would use this time to qualify as a coach and clinical hypnotherapist. I knew with an overwhelming certainty that I would be working with a niche client base, but it wasn't until I had had a particularly bad four-day migraine that I awoke to an intense intuitive knowing that women journeying through this stage in their lives would be the focus of my business.

My path led me to the wonderful Julie Anne Hart and the releasing of my iChannel. The wisdom I carry with me was now ready to be released. I felt as though I was coming home to something that I needed to explore and open up more to; that somehow, she was the next piece in my development.

Through my iChannel, I have been awakened to the reality of this time of great change that menopause brings. The more I have explored the real meaning of menopause, the more I am in awe of how powerful we truly are as women. What I thought was the beginning of the end is not true. I had 12 years of physical menopause symptoms, but for me, these were physical things I had to have to enable me to really see what we as women can embrace and use to empower us. My hot flushes were the releasing of buried emotions that needed to be addressed and released as hotness through my body. My menopause was not just a physical experience, it was also a healing of past mind and spiritual hurts that I had long buried.

From thinking I was moving to an 'ending', I was definitely moved to know that everything is a beginning, a renewal.

The word 'menopause' comes from the Greek words 'menos', meaning month, and 'pause', meaning to cease. It is a word in our modern world that we are being taught to fear, as indeed I was in fear. Fear that I had let my family down as I didn't have children. Fear that I would be left 'on the shelf' and not destined to have a marriage. When it comes to menopause, it is now regularly treated as though it were a medical condition, a deficiency disease. Yet periods aren't treated as a medical condition; periods are seen as a natural part of a girl maturing into the first part of her womanhood, into her fertile years. So why should menopause not be seen as a woman moving into the next cycle of her life? It is a natural part of a woman's growth to move from womanhood into her mid-life or crone years.

As you are reading this, you may have thought how unlucky I was to experience an early menopause. You may believe that for you, this event is many years away. However, if each of us takes a pause, removes our blindfold, and wakes up to the perception that we don't need to follow the mainstream of needing to medicate to get through menopause, we could see that this phase is another gateway to our growth, one that we should be preparing for all our lives.

Menopause is a powerhouse of our untapped potential, far beyond what society and our culture has ever spoken of openly in this modern world. Instead of welcoming this phase, we have become blind to its attributes and fear the rising of our inner genius and brilliance.

If we look back to our ancestors, we discover that within the culture at the time, they knew menopause was the time to engage with their personal power, with the power of the feminine. They knew it to be a time of learning, of understanding and celebrating all that they had experienced in their lives as women up to menopause. They celebrated all their life experiences and were open to releasing all the feelings, emotions, events and people that no longer served any purpose in their lives from this point onwards through the menopause. It was a rite of passage.

Through the subsequent years, we have been taught as women to hide and protect ourselves out of fear of persecution of our divine power.

Menopause is our journey to the next stage of self-discovery. It invites us to go deeper into ourselves and is our chance to look back at all our life experiences, our roadmap through life and take the time to honour that journey. It is time to celebrate and move into embracing our divine feminine power.

Sadly, most women these days remain blind to all this and enter this most powerful time in fear, overwhelm, stress and anxiety. Our mind leads the way, and our spirit is depressed, where we feel ill at ease with ourselves, bare and barren. We feel we are losing our role in this life, our identity that we have held onto for so long. We feel we are on a spiral downwards. We choose to batter and bruise ourselves with our words and our thoughts and through fear we repeat our patterns of "I'M NOT good enough, I DON'T feel worthy enough... I SHOULD

HAVE... I CAN'T..." instead of accepting and embracing who we are and standing in our power.

It is imperative through these times of change that we understand from a mind, body and spirit perspective about our own health and are able to manage these changes ahead, for we have all that we need within ourselves; our psyche has a gut knowing of what is right for us.

Menopause brings out all of a woman's skills and potential through helping her understand everything life has so far delivered to her. The messages and the meaning of menopause are found through the hotness you will be releasing, as it accesses your power, the creative fertility within. The anxiety you are experiencing is a fear of the future, the unknown calling you.

Where you may have experienced mediocrity in your life, you will have the opportunity to step into your magnificence. Where you have experienced blame, there is an opportunity to step into your brilliance. Any sadness you have felt through your life, there is an opportunity to step into success. If there has been any despair or depression that has touched you, there is an opportunity to step into self-discovery.

It is understanding your life's journey and releasing it from pain to gain. Releasing it from despair into discovery, releasing it from sadness into success. When you seek out your own map of meaning of the menopause, you will understand what needs to be released with the changes of your hormones, as this is the deeper meaning of the menopause.

By taking off your blindfold you will see, sense, feel and birth all that you truly are, and you will come into your spirit, your raw authenticness, your natural essence and your power.

In doing this, you are open to continued growth, expansion and ascension.

Self-healing can only occur when one makes a congruent decision to say:

*I desire to become.*
*I desire to heal.*
*I desire to have health.*
*I desire to live the best life.*

It is a discerned choice where you cannot have one foot in 'illness' and one foot in 'wellness'. Your purpose, power, potential and prosperity is at its highest form during these formative years and so to come into your power, you must address your health and wellbeing. Your total immersion to healing needs to fit into these next four steps to wellness. It needs to begin and be crafted into every breath, every thought, every perception you have from now on.

The only way to advance your physical health and wellbeing is to understand the truth and the miracle of this time and drop the myths.

As you heal, you will be working through doubts, fears and anxieties that crop up, and are naturally released.

You see, the biggest teacher, healer, coach and mentor is within yourself. It is within your DNA. Every answer to your life's journey is uniquely encoded within you. It is not in anyone else. It connects into your power. You can release the tears and the pain of the past and make the higher self that has, until now been laid dormant, active.

In order for a woman to claim her power, there are requirements to the reclaiming of what has been lost.

Those requirements are shaped around the whole of you, a holistic solution for your mind, your body, and your spirit.

Below are four suggested steps for you to take. If you commit to doing these on a regular basis, you can begin to clear your mind and have an active body that will sustain you and move your spirit to a more positive connection.

## Step 1: Your Deed of Commitment

Write a commitment deed to yourself, where you clearly detail what changes you are committing yourself to change. For example, my health and wellbeing take priority in my life. I continue to be active on a daily basis as for me, movement is not a chore; it improves my physical energy. On an inner level, I commit to a regular meditation practice as I am aware that this is self-care on another level that takes care of my mental, emotional and spiritual health.

This deed yields over 80% of your results. Through this, you will begin to understand the power you hold as a woman: the power of your mind, body and spirit, your strength, determination, perseverance, your consistency and continual commitment. This is also a time for you to hold a healing ceremony. This is a time to honour that commitment you have made to yourself; this is your first step on your rite of passage.

## Step 2: Changing Your Perception

The next step on your healing journey is perception. A woman's emotional health and wellbeing can decline or excel during this time depending on how she chooses to see her life and her life's experiences and how those life experiences have impacted on her health and wellbeing and her healing. You must move your perception into who you really are and what you have to offer and chose to embrace a positive spirit. This engages all your senses, for all that you see, hear, touch, taste and smell is what you will receive and is what you will become. Changing the thoughts and feelings you have about your past and how you experienced it ensures you raise your standards and your self-esteem as you progress forwards. However, it is also crucial that you see yourself at a higher level of perfection and see your past in the same light. You must be prepared to release any negativity so you heal.

When you look at this time as a change of perception, a change of energy, a change into more power, when it is looked at from a different perspective, there will be fewer physical symptoms that you experience. When all your life is looked at with honour and respect, and you don't dim or diminish your feminine essence within, there is less despair and depression and sadness and physical and emotional imbalance. Focus on past experiences that have graced your life and, during this part of your healing journey, change how you now view these experiences.

### Step 3: Sacred Space

Create for yourself a quiet space to retreat, a sacred space where you can pause and give yourself the potential to begin to heal and clear your mind. You will be going within to reflect, to seek deeper clarity, to seek deeper intent. Through this silence you can consolidate your commitment and move the perception you have of your life's experiences to begin to align your mind, body and spirit to greater health and wellness.

### Step 4: Wholeness

As you begin to allow and start to bring together all aspects of feminine power, you become congruent with each of these parts, each facet as they have always been interlinked and interconnected pieces that form wholeness. You must come to know, accept and embrace all these facets of yourself, honouring and owning these whole facets, these parts of you, all parts of your personality; facets of your prosperity that will birth your unique wholeness. When you acknowledge these facets, when you identify them, you must embrace them and take ownership of them, as you are emerging into your empowerment. It is a powerful healing that brings holistic wholeness of the self to a whole new level.

It is your brilliance that has lain dormant within you, that has always been there, for the skills and abilities are in you from birth. It is at this time of your rite of passage that, by taking a pause in order to access your whole self, you have the ability to birth your brilliance from within.

If as a woman you feel a dis-ease with your primal power, a separation from your success, a sadness to the truth of your spirit, or you wish to empower the potential from within, you are now able to expand and embrace all parts of your holistic health.

Healing is a continual, infinite journey. It's never finite. It never stops at a certain age because you are infinite in potential and purpose and prosperity and therefore the destination never exists.

If you are feeling a separation from your successes in life, a sadness to the truth of your spirit and wish to unleash your genius level of uniqueness, then you are ready to birth your brilliance.

And me? Where am I in this next stage of life?

By delving deep into the depths of myself, by making my own deed of commitment with a resolve to uncover what this time, this rite of passage means to me, I have moved through the layers of repression to the depths of my uniqueness, to a deep sense of who I am, and a deeper sense of the meaning of this time where I have discovered my real purpose in this life.

For the first time, I feel like a real adult, with the right to walk with the wisdom that I have earnt through my life's experiences, embracing my power from within. Menopause is NOT the ending that we are led to believe. Menopause is your next stage in life to lead you back to the woman you have always been and who you are truly meant to be.

# CHAPTER 11

# Life

OUR MAIN AIM FOR THIS book was that it gave you an insight into our lives, our adversities and how they led to our advancement. We hope it gives you a sense of connection, that even in our uniqueness we are not different from each other. We live, we experience life, we learn to deal with the emotions that arise, and we learn to accept, love and share, forever moving into more of our skills and talents for good.

How else can I conclude this book of insights other than to ask the spiritual channel that is open and accessible to me for guidance? That guidance is accessible to you too. I hope you find the words below support your next step.

With love and blessings from us all. xx

"Your eyes are akin to your spirit. Allow yourself to begin to see to acknowledge the spirit within you. When you live life in a way that is not separated from your own spirit and the infinite divine spirit, you are in connection with a divine power that will assist you and support you and, as you allow this magnificent energy force in, you will be guided by the highest most loving all-encompassing power.

"Great healing comes from building a greater relationship with yourself, with others that are akin to your soul, with purpose, with the planet and with the divine power that is always with you. The spirit is in the wind; it is your breath. The spirit is in the warmth of your body; it is the fire, the sunshine of your solar system, the gut of your knowing. Your emotions are like water, they are your life force energy; when you feel them, you flow upon life's journey easily. The earth is your happiness; the present moment is your wealth. You are everything when you know you need nothing because when everything presents itself, you are fulfilled. Wholeness requires a spiritual connection.

"Through life's losses and grief, you learn to feel, process and regain life's flow. The power of being able to introspect is the strength within you to go to the core of many emotions. The power of reflection brings healing, understanding and insight, strengthening the soul to live, leading you into life's destiny." - Sue Macdonald

"Your breath is a neutraliser of pain. Use it when you need to reach for more comfort and self-care. Breathe out and breathe in deep and slow and you will feel your own mind, body and spirit supporting you. Your body has its own language: listen to its guidance and lead from love." - Lucy Denver

"The power of experiencing life is the real education that no institution can provide. When you share from your soul, real life, real learning, you are working in realms of a deep spiritual connection. Such a connection ignites a confidence within you to move out of your familiar so you can begin to access the unknown." - Buckso Dillion

"The earth is a grid, a series of power lines that support the continuation of provision, protection and potential. You are akin to the earth: the same lines are within you, the same power is accessible. The self-provision, self-protection and potential is within you. Know your energy, know that ancient art of your grid. Activate it and advance." - Katy Henry

"We underestimate the power of our physical bodies. Your physical body holds the power of the spirit. When you move, it inspires the spirit to ignite the energy within you. When you move in a sacred way, you are speaking a universal language through the power of the body's movement." – Jacqui Moore

"Love is leadership. The love of your body, the love of wellbeing, the love to nurture the nature of your own physical and emotional needs enables you to become a magnet for manifestation. Such an attraction is the love you have for yourself. The vibe of love is your vortex energy that surrounds you. Become healthy and naturally wealthy." - Lucy West

"Nature's way is often discarded. The power of the body's cycle always gives the spirit a gift when you learn to return to the wisdom within. Everything is given as a gift; just like the seasons' cycles, it leads nature into an ever-unfolding cycle of rebirth." – Pam Bailey

# About the Authors

**Julie Anne Hart**

Julie Anne Hart is a spiritual conduit for the wisdom that is gifted to help us heal, grow, lead and love. Julie Anne works with the spiritual knowledge given to her to promote human potentiality and change.

Email: julie@julieannehart.com
Websites: www.beyondyourawareness
& www.ichannelwisdom.com

## Sue MacDonald

Through life's losses and grief, you learn to feel, process and regain life's flow. The power of being able to introspect is the strength within you to go to the core of many emotions. The power of reflection brings healing, understanding and insight. Strengthening the soul to live, and to be led into the fullness of life.

Email: sue@introspectandreflect.co.uk
Websites: https://introspectandreflect.co.uk/ & https://thecaramcdonaldfoundation.co.uk/

## Lucy Denver

Your breath is a neutraliser of pain. Use it when you need to reach for more comfort and self-care. Pause often to respect the breath in your body. Breathe in and breathe out deeply and slowly and you will feel your own body, mind and spirit supporting you. Your body has its own language: listen to its guidance and lead from compassion and kindness. The potential is within you when you understand how to use your own circuit of genius that leads to unending wellness.

Email: lucydenver@gmail.com
Website: wearetheantidote.co.uk
Social Media: @we_aretheantidote

## Buckso Dhillon-Woolley

Buckso specializes in the dissolution of trauma and decompression of the mind. As an Energy Healer, Performer and Mentor Buckso is now on a mission to share the wisdom and teachings, to inspire, motivate and encourage women ALL over the world, to embrace their TRUE essence, find their voice and ALWAYS live and speak, THEIR truth!

Email: bucksodw@gmail.com
Website: go.bucksodw.com
Instagram: www.instagram.com/thevibrantsage

## Katy Henry

The earth is a grid, a series of power lines that support the continuation of provision, protection and potential. You are akin to the earth. The same lines are within you. The same power is accessible. The self provision, self protection and potential is within you. Know your energy, know that ancient art of your grid. Activate it and advance. The power is yours, are you ready to claim it.

Email: katyhenryunlimited@gmail.com
Website: www.activateandadvance.co.uk

## Jacqueline Moore

Love is leadership, the love of your body, the love of well-being. The love to nurture the nature of your own physical and emotional needs enables you to become a magnet for manifestation. Such an attraction is the love you have for yourself. The vibe of love is your vortex energy that surrounds you. Become healthy and naturally wealthy through movement.

Email: hello@transformationalmovement.co.uk:
Website: www.transformationalmovement.co.uk

## Lucy West

Lucy West is passionate about helping people break free of yo-yo diet culture and truly embraces the concept of self-love. By educating clients on the importance of gut health and the spiritual practice of taking care of our bodies a transformational process occurs. Food, fun and freedom become the norm and restriction, guilt and punishment are off the table for good.

Email: lucywestvp@gmail.com
Website: lucywest.arbonne.com
Instagram: www.instagram.com/lucywestvp

## Pam Bailey

Pam helps in demystifying the mess of mainstream understanding that currently exists around the time of change at midlife for a woman, and helps them to come home to the power, the energy and the health that has been hidden within one's own psyche, consciousness, body, health, mind, and unique essence.

Email: info@changesahead.co.uk
Website: www.changesahead.co.uk
LinkedIn: https://linktr.ee/changesahead1therapies

Ingram Content Group UK Ltd.
Milton Keynes UK
UKHW021909200623
423774UK00010B/145

9 781739 723088